OPTIMAL COMMUNICATION

CSLI Lecture Notes
Number 177

OPTIMAL
COMMUNICATION

REINHARD BLUTNER
HELEN DE HOOP
PETRA HENDRIKS

CSLI
PUBLICATIONS
Center for the Study of
Language and Information
Stanford, California

Copyright © 2006
CSLI Publications
Center for the Study of Language and Information
Leland Stanford Junior University
Printed in the United States
10 09 08 07 06   1 2 3 4 5

Library of Congress Cataloging-in-Publication Data

Blutner, Reinhard.
Optimal communication /
by Reinhard Blutner, Helen de Hoop, and Petra Hendriks.

p. cm. – (CSLI lecture notes ; no. 177)

Includes bibliographical references and index.
ISBN 1-57586-514-9 (pbk. : alk. paper)
ISBN 1-57586-513-0 (cloth : alk. paper)

1. Optimality theory (Linguistics) 2. Pragmatics.
3. Grammar, Comparative and general—Syntax.
I. Hoop, Helen de, 1964– . II. Hendriks, Petra, 1964– .
III. Title. IV. Series.

P158.42.B58 2005
415–dc22   2005034367
CIP

CSLI was founded in 1983 by researchers from Stanford University, SRI
International, and Xerox PARC to further the research and development of
integrated theories of language, information, and computation. CSLI headquarters
and CSLI Publications are located on the campus of Stanford University.

CSLI Publications reports new developments in the study of language,
information, and computation. Please visit our web site at
http://cslipublications.stanford.edu/
for comments on this and other titles, as well as for changes
and corrections by the authors and publisher.

Contents

Acknowledgments

This book could not have been written without the help of many others. Helen de Hoop and Petra Hendriks thank the Netherlands Organisation for Scientific Research (NWO) for financial support of the NWO/Cognition project 'Conflicts in Interpretation', grant no. 051-02-070. Helen the Hoop also gratefully acknowledges NWO for the PIONIER project 'Case Cross-linguistically', grant no. 220-70-003.

We have benefited enormously from inspiring discussions with our colleagues, in particular Anton Benz, Gerlof Bouma, Henriëtte de Swart, Peter de Swart, Gerhard Jäger, Irene Krämer, Monique Lamers, Andrej Malchukov, Jason Mattausch, Jennifer Spenader, Henk Zeevat, and Joost Zwarts. Earlier versions of chapters have been used for a foundational course at the ESSLLI Summer School in Helsinki in 2001, for a course within the program of Artificial Intelligence at the University of Groningen in 2003 and 2004, and for a course during the LOT Winter School 2004 in Amsterdam.

We thank the participants of these courses for discussions and comments. Furthermore, many lively and insightful discussions took place during the Conference on the Optimization of Interpretation (January 2000, Utrecht), the Conference on Optimal Interpretations of Words and Constituents (August 2000, Utrecht), the workshop on Optimality Theory and Pragmatics (June 2002, Berlin), the workshop on Logic, Neural Networks, and Optimality Theory (July 2003, Berlin), and the KNAW Academy Colloquium on Cognitive Foundations of Interpretation (October 2004, Amsterdam). We are grateful to participants of these events for sharing their views on many fundamental and empirical issues with us.

Finally, we thank Dikran Karagueuzian of CSLI Publications for his support, an anonymous reviewer for many valuable comments, and Sander

Lestrade for his help with the editorial work. As for the inevitable errors in the book, what we would like to say about them is recoverable for the experienced reader and can therefore be omitted from this text.

Preface

Since the introduction of Optimality Theory (OT) into phonology by Alan Prince and Paul Smolensky in 1993, OT has had an enormous impact on the field of linguistics. Initially, OT was only applied to the linguistic sub-domains of phonology, morphology and syntax. Petra Hendriks and Helen de Hoop played a significant role in introducing OT into the sub-domain of semantics. They showed that OT is able to elucidate several issues in semantics pertaining to the syntax/semantics interface. Following the introduction of OT into the domain of natural language interpretation, Reinhard Blutner pointed out the necessity of bidirectional versions of OT for integrating formal pragmatics into OT. This book arose out of these two strands of research. The book argues for an optimization perspective on natural language interpretation and production which must be bidirectional in nature. By distinguishing between the perspective of the speaker and the perspective of the hearer, it is argued that the OT grammar is able to solve several, otherwise unexplained, semantic and pragmatic puzzles of language.

The book is addressed to researchers and students in linguistics, computational linguistics, and language acquisition, and might also be of interest to cognitive scientists, philosophers of mind, and researchers in artificial intelligence. The book aims at presenting the state of the art on OT and natural language interpretation. It gives an introduction to OT semantics and bidirectional OT, and contains cutting edge research results within this area. We hope this book will not only contribute to the general understanding of the human language faculty, but also help to bridge the gap between linguistics and other cognitive sciences.

Amsterdam/Nijmegen/Groningen, May 2005

1

Introduction

1.1 Optimality Theory as a Theory of Knowledge

When people try to convey their thoughts to each other via natural language, they usually succeed quite well. A plausible explanation is that people use some kind of system for building and interpreting sentences that is more or less the same for all speakers of the same language. The goal of linguistics is to specify this system of linguistic knowledge. This system of linguistic knowledge is usually called a **grammar**.

Possessing a grammar of the language enables speakers to interpret sentences they have never heard before. Even if you have never heard the sentence *Seven Spanish semanticists drank beer in a bar in Berlin*, you will nevertheless be able to interpret this sentence if you possess sufficient knowledge of English. Speakers of a language are also able to produce sentences they have never heard before. It is not difficult to think up a sentence in your native language that nobody has ever spoken to you. Finally, speakers of a language are able to tell whether a given form is a possible expression in the language or not. Is the form *bfli* a possible word of English? Most speakers of English would say no, although they would consider the very similar form *flib* a possible word of English.

So speakers of a language are assumed to possess a grammar of the language they speak. What does this grammar look like? This is not an easy question to answer. There are in principle infinitely many forms that such a grammar could take. If we want to construct a grammar, we have to decide on the content of the rules that make up the grammar. Grammars can also differ in the type of rules. Therefore, we also have to make a decision about the required complexity of the rules and about their form. With respect to the latter point, we could decide that all rules must be *if-then* rules or that all rules must be negative rules prohibiting the cooccurrence of certain features. Grammars can also differ in the function of the rules. The rules may be generative and generate all and only all expressions of the language, or they may behave as filters eliminating ungrammatical expressions. Moreover, grammars can differ in the way the rules interact. Rules may apply one after the other (i.e., in a derivational way) or they may apply simultaneously (i.e., in a parallel way). Certain rules may apply before other rules or be more important than other rules, resulting in a modular architecture of the grammar. Alternatively, all rules may have the same status.

These are only a few of the ways in which grammars can differ. Grammars may differ in many more respects. Some scientists claim that linguistic knowledge does not involve any rules at all but merely is the ability to associate patterns of a certain kind with patterns of another kind. How do we know which grammar is the correct one for specifying a certain language? This is part of linguistic research. One of the criteria for determining whether a grammar is the correct one is its ability to distinguish between the **possible forms** and the **impossible forms** of a particular language. If you are a native speaker of a language, you are able to make this distinction. Therefore, a grammar must be evaluated with respect to how well it can make this distinction. Similarly, as a speaker of a language you know which possible meanings a given sentence can have in that language and which meanings are not possible for that sentence. For example, the English sentence *Kim did* can mean that Kim drank beer, given an appropriate context such as a preceding question *Who drank beer?* In another linguistic context, it can mean that Kim went to Groningen. But the sentence *Kim did* can never mean that all linguists like beer. A grammar should therefore be able to also make the distinction between **possible meanings** and **impossible meanings** for a given form.

If you speak one language, this does not mean that you have knowledge of all existing languages. There are about 5000 languages spoken all over the world. These languages differ in a number of respects. But they also share a number of properties. Because languages are related to one another and are used for the same functions, their grammars are assumed not to differ too much. Another important criterion for deciding which grammar is the correct one therefore is whether the grammar is able to explain the range and type of properties languages share and the range and type of variation possible between languages. In other words, a grammar should explain the nature of **language universals** and **language variation**.

Other criteria for the evaluation of grammars are learnability, psychological plausibility and neurological plausibility. A grammar is a specification of the system of linguistic knowledge that a speaker of the language has. This knowledge has to end up in the mind of a speaker somehow. This means that the grammar has to be compatible with a theory of learning this grammar. In addition, the grammar must be compatible with psychological views on knowledge representation and knowledge processing. Linguistic knowledge does not just sit in the mind of a speaker. Rather, it is actively used by the speaker. Therefore, psychological plausibility is an important criterion as well. Finally, the knowledge a speaker has of the grammar resides in the brain. The grammar must therefore also be compatible with properties of, and processes in, the brain. So we can formulate at least five criteria for evaluating a grammar: (1) the ability to distinguish between possible and impossible forms and meanings, (2) the ability to explain patterns across languages, (3) learnability, (4) psychological plausibility, and (5) neurological plausibility. Because we want to construct a model of the linguistic knowledge that speakers of natural languages have, these five criteria will play a role throughout the book.

In this book, we focus on a linguistic theory known as **Optimality Theory**. Optimality Theory is a possible model of the system of linguistic knowledge a speaker of a language possesses. In the next section, the basic concepts of Optimality Theory are introduced. It is shown here how Optimality Theory accounts for the actual forms and meanings of a language, and for language universals and language variation. In later chapters, issues of learnability and psychological and neurological plausibility will be discussed, although we will already touch upon a few related aspects in the present chapter.

1.2 Basic Concepts of OT

It is quite easy to come up with general tendencies that hold for observable properties of a given language. For example, sentences in English usually have a subject. The subject often is the first element in the sentence. In many cases, the subject is the agent of the action expressed by the verb. Crucially, however, these statements are mere tendencies, not absolute laws. It is very difficult to find observable properties that always hold without exception in a given language. If we were to formulate these general statements as rules, these rules would often have to be broken because of a number of exceptions.

In Optimality Theory (henceforth 'OT'), these general statements take the form of **violable constraints**. Because these constraints express very general statements with respect to the language, they can be in conflict. Conflicts among constraints are resolved because the constraints differ in strength. The constraints can be ordered in a **constraint hierarchy** according to strength. A constraint may be violated, but only in order to satisfy a stronger constraint. A grammar is thus assumed to consist of a ranked set of violable constraints. A general assumption within OT is that languages share the same set of constraints. Differences between languages arise from the language-particular ranking of the same set of constraints.

OT specifies the relation between an input and an output. This relation is mediated by two formal mechanisms, **GEN** and **EVAL**. GEN (for Generator) creates possible output candidates on the basis of a given input. EVAL (for Evaluator) uses the language-specific constraint ranking of the universal set of constraints (**CON**) to select the best candidate for a given input from among the **candidate set** produced by GEN.

In phonology, the **input** to this process of optimization is an underlying linguistic representation. The **output** is the form as it is expressed. As a simple example, consider the process of syllabification. Words in all languages are composed of syllables. Speakers of a language know how to break up words in their language into syllables. In English, for example, the word *balcony* is syllabified as *bal.co.ny*, and the word *palace* as *pa.lace*. The dots refer to syllable boundaries. To account for the process of syllabification, the input must be an unsyllabified string of sound segments. The output of this process of optimization must be a syllabified string.

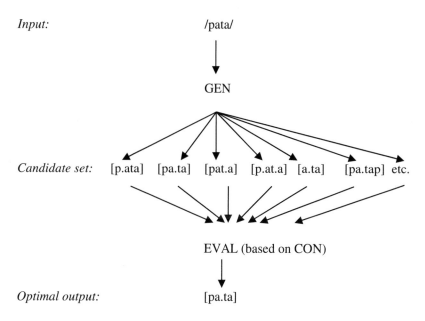

Input: /pata/

GEN

Candidate set: [p.ata] [pa.ta] [pat.a] [p.at.a] [a.ta] [pa.tap] etc.

EVAL (based on CON)

Optimal output: [pa.ta]

Figure 1 The basic architecture of Optimality Theory (adapted from Archangeli & Langendoen, 1997))

Given an unsyllabified string of sound segments such as /pata/ as the input, GEN generates a set of possible syllabifications for this string. Following phonological conventions, symbols between slashes represent the underlying speech segments. Symbols between square brackets represent the actual speech sounds. From a set of possible output candidates, EVAL selects the candidate that best satisfies the ranked set of constraints for that language. This candidate is the output form which is expressed. The way this output form is syllabified corresponds best to the constraints of the language, although it might not satisfy all constraints. In the next section, some of the constraints involved in syllabification are discussed.

Note that the candidate set created by GEN must be infinite. Because new elements can be added to the string of sound segments, as in the sixth candidate in Figure 1 ([pa.tap]), in principle infinitely many candidates are possible for any given input string. This property poses serious problems for computational models of OT. In addition, it is of course psychologically highly implausible. However, efforts have been made to circumvent this problem. For example, smart computational strategies might eliminate suboptimal candidates as a group rather than on a one-by-one basis. As soon as a candidate has been excluded due to its violation of some constraint, all other candidates that violate this constraint even more severely can also be excluded. Alternatively, the candidate set may be infinite in principle but finite in practice, bounded by cognitive principles. This result can be obtained by a computational model that adaptively generates and evaluates a finite number of candidates (Misker & Anderson, 2003). Although only a finite number of candidates are generated, in principle any candidate could be generated this way, thus accounting for the infinity of the candidate set.

1.3 Language Universals and Language Variation

In OT, the output is determined through optimization over a ranked set of constraints. Moreover, variation among languages follows from differences in constraint rankings. In this section, we will illustrate this property of OT by presenting an example of syllabification in different languages (cf. Archangeli, 1997).

Words are composed of syllables. Syllables are structured strings of sounds. They can have an onset (one or more consonants at the beginning of the syllable, a peak (usually a vowel) and a coda (one or more consonants at the end of the syllable). If you look at syllables across languages, a number of general properties can be observed with respect to the structure of syllables. Often, syllables begin with a consonant. Usually, the center of a syllable is a vowel. Syllables ending with a consonant are less common than syllables ending with a vowel. Thus, the typical syllable is of the form CV (consonant-vowel). These general statements can be formulated as violable constraints:

(1) ONSET: Syllables begin with a consonant.
PEAK: Syllables have one vowel.
NOCODA: Syllables end with a vowel.
*COMPLEX: Syllables have at most one consonant at an edge.

The fourth constraint, *COMPLEX, states that consonant clusters are dispreferred. The symbol '*' is used by linguists to indicate unacceptability. If it is placed in front of a sentence, it indicates that the sentence is unacceptable. If it is placed in front of the name of a constraint, it indicates that the constraint prohibits a certain pattern. In the case of *COMPLEX, the constraint prohibits the occurrence of consonant clusters. But because the constraint is a violable constraint, consonant clusters may occur if this allows the syllable to satisfy a stronger constraint.

These constraints are members of the family of **markedness** constraints. The term markedness is used in linguistics to refer to the fact that certain properties are found in virtually all languages whereas other properties are found quite rarely. Properties which are found in many or all languages are unmarked properties. If a property is very rare across languages, on the other hand, it is a highly marked property. Because OT constraints express general statements with respect to language, markedness is encoded via constraints and constraint violations. Violation of a constraint results in a more marked form with respect to the property referred to by the constraint. Constraint satisfaction, on the other hand, corresponds to unmarked properties. Markedness constraints have the effect that you cannot always express the underlying form exactly as it is given. As a result, certain linguistic forms are preferred to other forms. Note that markedness constraints refer to the form of the output only and are blind to the form of the input.

In addition to markedness constraints, OT also has **faithfulness** constraints. OT specifies a relation between an input and an output. Faithfulness constraints state that the input must be identical to the output. In other words, faithfulness constraints promote that you express the underlying form. Whereas markedness constraint only take into account the output, faithfulness constraints take into account both the input and the output. In contrast to derivational approaches to language such as classical generative phonology or generative syntax, in OT there are no constraints that exclusively refer to the input. Violations of faithfulness constraints lead to differences between input and output. These differences might be connected to different aspects of the input and output, for example to the consonants in the input and output, or to the vowels in the input and output:

(2) FAITHC: Consonants in the input must be in the output and vice versa.
FaithV: Vowels in the input must be in the output and vice versa.

There is an inherent tension between markedness constraints and faithfulness constraints. Whereas faithfulness constraints promote identity between input and output, markedness constraints sometimes promote a difference between input and output because they favor specific output forms (such as, for example, syllables ending with a vowel). So the constraints in OT potentially **conflict**. From a functional point of view, one could say that markedness constraints exert pressure towards unmarked forms, which may be easier to articulate or perceive, whereas faithfulness constraint preserve contrasts in form, making it possible to have distinct forms to express different meanings.

With the constraints introduced here, it is possible to do a small linguistic thought experiment. In virtually all languages, it is possible to construct new words by combining two morphemes. Morphemes are the smallest meaningful units in a language. Morphemes can be words (for example, the word *word* is a morpheme), but morphemes can also be smaller units than words. The plural inflection marker –*s*, as in *words*, also is a morpheme, as are the prefix *un-* in *unhappy* and the suffix –*ness* in *happiness*. If we combine two morphemes to build a new word, we can investigate how the sounds making up this new word behave. If we take a first morpheme ending on two consonants and a second morpheme beginning with a consonant, we have suddenly created a conflict between the constraints we just introduced. It is impossible to place syllable boundaries in such a way that the resulting syllables completely satisfy all constraints. Now let us see how different languages solve this conflict.

Let us start our small experiment with English. Combining the adjective *damp* with the suffix –*ness*, we have three consonants in a row: the /m/ and the /p/ of *damp* and the /n/ of -*ness*. This is in conflict with the constraint *COMPLEX, which prohibits consonant clusters. Nevertheless, the new word *dampness* is pronounced with all three consonants in place. Apparently, in English the constraint *COMPLEX is ranked lower than the other constraints on syllable structure. A common way to illustrate the interaction among constraints in OT is by means of a **tableau**. Consider the following tableau:

TABLEAU 1
Syllabification in English

Input: /damp-nɛs/	FAITHV	PEAK	FAITHC	*COMPLEX
☞ damp.nɛs				*
dam.nɛs			*!	
dam.pi.nɛs	*!			
dam.p.nɛs		*!		

The top left-hand cell in the tableau presents the input representation for which candidates are being considered. A number of candidates are given in the leftmost column. These candidates are in **competition** with each other. Only the candidate that satisfies the constraints best, i.e. the optimal candidate, is pronounced. The constraints are ranked across the top, going from the highest ranked constraint on the left to the lowest ranked constraint on the right. Dashed lines between constraints indicate that the ranking is not determined or is not relevant. Solid lines between constraints indicate relevant rankings. In Tableau 1, the constraint *COMPLEX is ranked lower than the constraints FAITHV, PEAK and FAITHC. The relative ranking of these latter three constraints is not relevant. This can be expressed as follows: {FAITHV, PEAK, FAITHC} » *COMPLEX. In other words, the constraints FAITHV, PEAK and FAITHC each **dominate** the constraint *COMPLEX. For simplification, the constraints ONSET and NOCODA are left out of the tableau. All candidates in the tableau satisfy these two constraints. An asterisk (*) in a cell indicates a violation of a constraint. An exclamation mark (!) indicates a fatal violation, i.e., a violation that renders this candidate suboptimal. The optimal candidate is indicated by the pointing hand (☞).

The **optimal candidate** is the candidate with the fewest violations of the higher-ranked constraints. In Tableau 1, this is the candidate *damp.nεs*. This candidate only violates the lowest ranked constraint *COMPLEX. The coda of the first syllable of this candidate is formed by two consonants, which is prohibited by *COMPLEX. However, violation of this constraint is not fatal. All other candidates violate one of the higher ranked constraints. For example, the second candidate violates FAITHC. A consonant present in the input representation (namely the /p/) does not appear in the candidate output. Deleting a consonant is therefore not the best solution in English for the problem posed by the three consonants in the input. In the third candidate, the vowel /i/ is added. Because this vowel is not present in the input, this candidate violates FAITHV. The fourth candidate, finally, violates the constraint PEAK. In this candidate, the consonant /p/ is syllabified by itself. English, however, does not allow for syllables without vowels. Thus, the English solution to the problem posed by three consonants in the input is to allow for complex consonant clusters. As a result, the input is identical to the output.

In Yawelmani, a Native American language that was once spoken in California, such a conflict is resolved differently. This can be illustrated by combination of the verb root *logw-* ('pulverize') with the suffix *–hin*, which is a marker of the past tense. Again, we have three consonants in a row. Yawelmani solves this conflict by adding a vowel (epenthesis). So in this example, the output differs from the input. This is illustrated in the following tableau:

TABLEAU 2
Syllabification in Yawelmani

Input: /logw-hin/	*COMPLEX	FAITHC	PEAK	FAITHV
logw.hin	*!			
log.whin	*!			
log.w.hin			*!	
log.hin		*!		
☞ lo.giw.hin				*

The first and second candidate are suboptimal because they violate the constraint *COMPLEX. Apparently, in Yawelmani this constraint is stronger than in English. In Yawelmani, it is not possible to have more than one consonant at the edge of a syllable (i.e., in its coda or in its onset), in contrast to English. But if complex consonant clusters are not possible, some other solution must be found for the problem of the three consonants. In Yawelmani, the solution is to add a vowel. This results in the optimal output *lo.giw.hin*. Thus, constraint FAITHV may be violated, but only in order to satisfy stronger constraints. *COMPLEX is such a stronger constraint. FAITHC and PEAK must also be stronger than FAITHV. Otherwise, it should have been possible in Yawelmani to delete a consonant or to syllabify a consonant by itself. This, however, is not an option in Yawelmani.

Now let us turn to Spanish for the third part of our linguistic thought experiment. In Spanish, it is possible to form a new word by combining the verb root *absorb-* with the adjective-forming suffix *–to*. The result is a string of two consonants, /r/ and /b/, followed by a third consonant, /t/. What is the Spanish solution to the problem of the three consonants? As Tableau 3 shows, in Spanish a consonant is deleted.

TABLEAU 3
Syllabification in Spanish

Input: /absorb-to/	FAITHV	PEAK	*COMPLEX	FAITHC
☞ ab.sor.to				*
ab.sorb.to			*!	
ab.sor.be.to	*!			
ab.sor.b.to		*!		

Spanish does not allow for violations of *COMPLEX. In this way, Spanish resembles Yawelmani. However, Spanish does not allow a vowel to be added either. Thus, the candidate *ab.sor.be.to* is suboptimal because there is a better candidate that does not violate FAITHV. This better candidate is *ab.sor.to*. This candidate violates FAITHC, but this is allowed because it is the only way to satisfy the other, stronger, constraints.

The final language we will look at for our thought experiment is Berber, a language spoken in Morocco. In Berber, it is possible to create a three consonant sequence by combining the verb *fsi* ('untie') with the third person feminine singular prefix *t-*. The Berber solution to the three consonant problem is to allow for a syllable without a vowel:

TABLEAU 4
Syllabification in Berber

Input: /t-fsi/	FAITHV	*COMPLEX	FAITHC	PEAK
t.fsi		*!		*
.si			*!*	
f.si			*!	*
t.si			*!	*
tif.si	*!			
☞ tf.si				*

As in the other languages that participated in our thought experiment, every candidate in Berber violates at least one constraint. Creating a single syllable with the prefix /t/ violates *COMPLEX. Deleting one or more consonants violates FAITHC (every deletion of a consonant is counted as one violation). Adding a vowel violates FAITHV. Creating a syllable from the prefix and the first consonant of the verb violates PEAK. This candidate, in which a consonant is syllabified as a syllable peak, is the optimal one in Berber. This means that in Berber, PEAK is ranked lowest. Thus, Berber words do not need to contain vowels.

Our thought experiment showed that if we create a conflict among constraints, languages can resolve this conflict in different ways. Assuming that all languages can be described by the same set of constraints, resolution of the conflict was shown to depend on the relative ranking of these constraints. Observed differences between languages can thus be explained as the result of a different ranking of the same set of constraints. But more importantly: we can also make predictions about possible and impossible languages on the basis of our constraints. If there are four constraints, there are 4! possible constraint rankings. However, not all differences between constraint rankings correspond to observable differences between languages. From the possible constraint rankings, we can predict the types of languages that are possible. Also, we can predict which languages are imaginable but are nevertheless impossible. This is called **typology by reranking**. For example, it is imaginable that a language exists in which all consonants are placed in the beginning of the syllable and all vowels at the end of the syllable. However, such a language would never arise from a reranking of the constraints that were introduced in this chapter. From these constraints, we predict such a language not to be possible.

Summarizing, OT explains language universals by the assumption that languages must be described by the same set of constraints, CON. Language variation arises as a result of a different, language-specific, ranking of these constraints.

1.4 A Brief History of OT

The historical roots of Optimality Theory lie in neural network modeling. In neural network modeling, computations are performed by a network of artificial neurons which is modeled after the human brain. A neural network consists of artificial neurons, or units, and multiple connections between these units. The input to a network consists of a fixed pattern of activation. Activation then flows through the network to construct an output pattern of activation. The neural network thus maps a specific input pattern to a specific output pattern. Crucial for this mapping are the concepts of Harmony and Harmony maximization, or optimization. The **Harmony** of a pattern of activation is a measure of its degree of conformity to the connections between the units in the network (Smolensky, 1986). Connections can be excitatory and have a positive weight, or inhibitory and have a negative weight. In addition, the greater the weight of a connection, the greater its importance to the outcome. The connections can be thought of as embodying various constraints. These constraints typically conflict. A pattern of activation that maximizes Harmony (or, minimizes energy) is one that optimally balances the demands of all the constraints in the network.

These ideas found their way into linguistics when it was realized that this concept of Harmony maximization in neural network modeling could be applied to theories of grammar as well (cf. Legendre, Miyata, & Smolensky, 1990a, 1990b; Prince & Smolensky, 1993, 1997). The result was a theory called Harmonic Grammar. At the heart of this theory lies the view that a grammar is a set of violable and potentially conflicting constraints that apply to combinations of linguistic elements. These constraints vary in strength. A grammatical structure is then one that optimally satisfies the total set of constraints defined by the grammar. In Harmonic Grammar, as in artificial neural networks, constraints are weighted. Through a process of summation, the overall effect of the total set of constraints can be determined. Optimality Theory is the non-numerical successor of Harmonic Grammar. In OT, it is generally assumed that **strict domination** holds over the rankings. This means that any higher-ranked constraint takes absolute priority over any lower-ranked constraint. A single violation of a higher-ranked constraint is always worse than any number of violations of any number of lower-ranked constraints. Lower-ranked constraints can never 'team up' against a higher-ranked constraint. Therefore, in OT, in contrast to Harmonic Grammar, there are no cumulative effects.

By incorporating core concepts from neural network modeling, OT thus appears to provide a way of integrating the subsymbolic level of the brain with the symbolic level that seems necessary for the description and explanation of cognitive processes. OT can be viewed as a higher-level theory of the computations that take place at the lower-level of neural networks. Optimization over discrete, symbolic representations does not need to be stipulated as some *ad hoc* property of the grammar but is derived from the numerical, continuous optimization that takes place at the level of neural processing. Of course, artificial neural networks are merely crude idealizations of the actual neural networks that make up the human brain. Nevertheless, because of the similarities between optimization in OT and optimization in artificial neural networks, an optimization approach to language seems to fare better with respect to the criterion of **neurological plausibility** than does a derivational approach adopting non-violable rules.

OT emerged as a linguistic theory in the early nineties. At the University of Arizona Phonology Conference in Tucson in April 1991, Alan Prince and Paul Smolensky presented a paper entitled 'Optimality'. This was followed two years later, in 1993, by a pair of manuscripts: *Optimality Theory: Constraint Interaction in Generative Grammar* by Alan Prince and Paul Smolensky, and *Prosodic Morphology I: Constraint Interaction and Satisfaction* by John McCarthy and Alan Prince. These papers received a lot of attention and since their appearance research in OT has grown enormously. In phonology, OT has become the dominant paradigm. In the areas of morphology and syntax, the influence of OT is increasing. And recently, OT is also being applied within the domains of semantics and pragmatics.

One of the reasons why OT caught on so rapidly in phonology is the fact that counterexamples could always be found to every formal model of phonological representation. Moreover, constraints were already being used in phonology, although these constraints were viewed as inviolable. See Archangeli (1997) for a discussion of this theoretical shift in phonology. In syntax, a search for universal principles has gone on for several decades.

However, the inviolability of the proposed syntactic principles could only be maintained at the cost of parameterization and built-in restrictions, so it seemed. Assuming syntactic rules to be violable might therefore offer a fruitful alternative. For pragmatics, the situation was more or less similar to phonology. As Blutner and Zeevat (2004) show, the idea of optimization was present in pragmatics right from the beginning. Because the line between semantics and pragmatics is not very clear-cut, the step to optimization in semantics was only a small one.

Let us look in somewhat more detail at the rules in syntax. In the currently dominant view of syntax known as Principles and Parameters Theory, whose most recent version is called the Minimalist Program (Chomsky, 1995), all languages are assumed to share a core of inviolable principles and differ syntactically as a result of how certain details of each principle are stated (parameterization). Speas (1997) lists the most important inviolable syntactic principles and makes explicit the hedges that are necessary to cover all cases. For example, the principle Satisfy says that all syntactic features must be satisfied (the essence of the principle). However, these features must be satisfied overtly if they are strong but covertly at Logical Form if they are weak (its hedge). Whether features are strong or weak depends on the language and is thus a parameterized property. This allows the theory to explain why in certain languages overt movement seems to be obligatory, whereas in other languages there does not seem to be any movement. In the latter cases, covert movement is assumed. We will return to issues regarding syntactic movement in the next chapter.

Other examples of inviolable principles which need hedges are the principle of Full Interpretation and the Extended Projection Principle. The principle of Full Interpretation says that there can be no superfluous symbols in a representation (the essence of the principle), except symbols which are deleted before the interface level (its hedge). This principle states that every lexical item in a sentence must contribute to the interpretation of that sentence. The Extended Projection Principle states that all clauses must have a subject (the essence of the principle), except for languages which lack overt expletives (its hedge). Expletives are elements such as *it* in the sentence *It is raining* and *there* in the sentence *There are three cats on the porch*, which do not have any independent meaning. In Principles and Parameters Theory, the presence of expletives is explained by saying that expletives delete right before the point at which they are semantically interpreted. So both the principle of Full Interpretation and the Extended Projection Principle must have some built-in restrictions. In fact, every one of the principles in current syntactic theory contains some sort of proviso, Speas claims. Apparently, it is impossible to find inviolable syntactic rules that do not have exceptions or built-in restrictions.

The interaction between the principle of Full Interpretation and the Extended Projection Principle seems to lend itself nicely to an OT treatment. The principle of Full Interpretation and the Extended Projection Principle can easily be reformulated as violable constraints. The violable version of the inviolable Extended Projection Principle is usually called SUBJECT:

(3) SUBJECT: Clauses must have a subject.
   FULL-INT: Constituents in the output must be interpreted.

A conflict between these two constraints arises if the meaning of the main verb of the sentence does not imply that there must be a subject. An example of such a verb is *to rain*. This verb does not require an argument which performs or undergoes some action, that is, it does not select for a thematic argument. So semantically, there is no need for a subject. However, the constraint SUBJECT expresses the syntactic requirement that sentences must have a subject. So what do we do in this case? Do we leave out the subject or do we insert a meaningless word to fill the subject position? In languages such as English, the constraint SUBJECT ranks above the constraint FULL-INT. Therefore, FULL-INT may be violated in order to satisfy SUBJECT. In other words, because it is more important in English to have a subject in the sentence than to have only meaningful words in the sentence, the English solution to the conflict is to allow for a meaningless element to fill the subject position. This element is the expletive *it*.

TABLEAU 5
Subjects in English

Input: 'It rains'	SUBJECT	FULL-INT
☞ It rains		*
Rains	*!	

Let us assume for the moment that the input to optimization in syntax is a meaning. The candidate outputs are possible forms for this meaning. Although the candidate set is potentially infinite, we have listed only the two most relevant candidates in Tableau 5: the candidate with an expletive subject and the candidate without a subject. Because the candidate with an expletive subject only violates the weaker constraint, this candidate is the optimal way to express the given meaning in English.

In languages such as Italian, on the other hand, it is more important to have only meaningful words in the sentence than to have a subject. The Italian solution to the conflict therefore is to leave out the subject.

TABLEAU 6
Subjects in Italian

Input: 'It rains'	FULL-INT	SUBJECT
EXPL piove	*!	
☞ Piove		*

EXPL stands for 'expletive'. Since Italian does not have a counterpart to English *it*, there is no lexical item we can put here. However, this is not the reason that the first candidate is unacceptable in Italian. If the constraint SUBJECT were strongest in Italian as well, some element would have been drafted to serve as an expletive, according to Grimshaw and Samek-Lodovici (1998).

As was pointed out above, it does not seem possible to find inviolable principles for syntactic structure. There are always exceptions and restrictions. OT permits constraints to be violated, thus allowing for exceptions to general statements. A form need not be unacceptable merely because it violates one or more of the constraints. Its acceptability also depends on how well it behaves with respect to other constraints. Constraint violations are allowed, but only if there is no way to construct an output that satisfies all constraints. In this case, violation of weaker constraints is preferred to violation of stronger constraints, and fewer violations are preferred to more violations of the same constraint. Because English and Italian differ in what is the weaker constraint, these languages have different optimal solutions to the conflict posed by the input and the constraints. The candidate output that satisfies the constraints best is the optimal output. This need not be a candidate that satisfies all constraints.

In addition to violability of constraints, competition plays a central role in OT. Well-formedness of candidates is not determined independently of other candidates. Rather, the well-formedness of a candidate depends on how well other, competing, candidates satisfy the constraints. As we saw earlier, the form *damp.nes* is acceptable because it is better than all other candidates. There is no other candidate that behaves equally well with respect to the other constraints and also satisfies *COMPLEX. On the other hand, the form *damp.er* is not a well-formed result of combining the adjective *damp* and the comparative suffix *-er*. Even though the first syllable in *damp.er* is completely identical to the first syllable in *damp.nes*, the first form is nevertheless unacceptable because there is a form that satisfies the constraints better, namely *dam.per*. This form does not violate the constraint *COMPLEX. The [m] forms the coda of the first syllable, while the [p] forms the onset of the second syllable, so there is no complex consonant cluster. Because the form *dam.per* does not violate any of the stronger constraints either, it is the optimal form. This illustrates that output forms are not evaluated independently, but always in comparison with other candidate outputs. In some cases, violation of a constraint leads to unacceptability, whereas in other cases, violation of the same constraint is allowed because it is the best option.

Interestingly, competition also appears to play a role in the Minimalist Program. Here, an important role is played by principles of **economy**. These principles mandate that any derivation or representation be maximally economical. If there is a choice between different derivations, the derivation should be chosen that is maximally economical. For example, movement should involve as few steps as possible. Also, movement should be to the closest possible landing site. Furthermore, the distance between two syntactically related elements should be as short as possible. In OT, economy plays an important role as well. Here, principles of economy take the form of constraints with respect to the structure of the utterance which penalize movement and other constraints which penalize the postulation of morphological or syntactic structure. In general, there seems to be agreement on the view that at least certain aspects of syntactic structure are subject to competition. This seems to do justice to the idea that language users do not strive to find the perfect linguistic solution for their goal but just settle for the best solution available, given the often highly conflicting demands that are placed on linguistic forms and meanings.

The possibility of avoiding inviolable rules (for which there does not seem to be any evidence at all, cf. Speas (1997)) and the view that there is competition among candidate outputs have made OT a highly attractive theoretical framework in different subdomains of linguistics. Many papers on OT are currently accessible in electronic form at the Rutgers Optimality Archive (ROA) at http://roa.rutgers.edu/. For example, Prince and Smolensky's (1993) manuscript can be downloaded from this site (ROA number 537-0802), as well as McCarthy and Prince's (1993) manuscript (ROA number 482-1201). Several other important papers on OT can be found here as well. The ROA is perhaps the most extensive electronic archive in linguistics.

1.5 Optimization of Interpretation

In Section 1.3, we presented an example from phonology (syllabification in four different languages), and in Section 1.4, we presented an example from syntax (the presence of subjects in English and Italian). In this section, we will present an example from semantics. But before we do that, let us first consider the nature of the input and the output that must be assumed for these different processes of optimization.

In the phonological example regarding syllabification, the input to the process of optimization was assumed to be an underlying phonological form, for example /damp-nɛs/. This input form is composed of two morphemes, the root *damp* and the suffix *-ness*. The underlying forms of these morphemes, /damp/ and /-nɛs/, are taken from the lexicon. The lexicon contains all contrastive properties of morphemes, including their phonological, morphological, syntactic, and semantic properties. No constraints are assumed to hold at this level of underlying forms, because in OT constraints never apply to input forms. This is termed the **richness of the base**.

An important question from a learning perspective concerns the way in which this lexicon with its underlying forms is learned. In order to build a lexicon, a learner must somehow be able to infer the underlying form of a morpheme on the basis of the surface form the learner encounters. Since there are no constraints on the input, it is easy to construct multiple inputs that result in the same output. Which of these inputs is the best one? It has been proposed that if several different inputs produce the same output, the input should be selected that incurs the least serious constraint violations on the output. That is, in the absence of empirical evidence for one underlying form over another, the input should be selected that is the closest to the output, because this choice minimizes the violation of faithfulness. This strategy is called **lexicon optimization** (Prince & Smolensky, 1993). Lexicon optimization thus is a way of selecting an input from a set of inputs producing the same output.

The lexicon provides the input specifications which are submitted to GEN. As we saw, GEN may add phonemes to the input, delete phonemes from the input, and add syllable boundaries. In general, GEN may posit any amount of structure, as long as it uses licit elements of linguistic representation, such as segmental structure (features and their grouping below the level of the segment), prosodic structure (syllable, prosodic word, etc.), morphological structure (root, stem, affix, etc.), and syntactic structure (X-bar structure, heads, specifiers, complements, etc.) (see Kager, 1999: 20). The output to the process of optimization is assumed to be a structured form, in our example: [damp.nɛs].

So, in phonology, both the input and output are forms. If we consider other aspects of language such as its syntax or its semantics, the input and output to the process of optimization must differ. For simplicity, when discussing the syntactic example regarding the presence of subjects in English and Italian, we assumed the input to be the intended meaning of the sentence. In studies on OT syntax such as Grimshaw (1997), however, the input to syntactic optimization is assumed to consist of a lexical head with a mapping of its argument structure into other lexical heads, plus a specification of other information such as tense. For example, to create the sentence *What did Mary say?*, the input is as in (4).

(4)   Input for the sentence *What did Mary say?* (cf. Grimshaw, 1997):

$say(x,y)$
$x = Mary$
$y = what$
$tense = past$

The presence of elements such as auxiliaries in the output and the order of the lexical elements result from the interaction among violable syntactic constraints. To account for the fact that competing candidates must be truth-functionally equivalent, Grimshaw (1997) has to add this as an additional assumption. In syntax, GEN has so far been assumed to generate only candidate structures that respect X-bar theory principles (Legendre, 2001), thus in effect taking X-bar theory to be a system of inviolable constraints, or a property of GEN. There are a number of operations that GEN may perform on the input, while obeying X-bar theory. GEN may introduce projections, functional heads such as auxiliaries and complementizers, empty elements such as traces, and coindexations. In addition, GEN may move lexical elements. The candidates generated by GEN are evaluated at the level of surface structure. The output of this process of syntactic optimization is a well-formed, structured sentence, for example [$_{CP}$ what did$_i$ [$_{IP}$ Mary e$_i$ [$_{VP}$ say t]]].

Because competing candidates are assumed to be semantically equivalent, the central question in OT syntax seems to be: Given a certain meaning, what is its optimal form? Applying OT to the domain of interpretation, we could formulate a closely related question for OT semantics: Given a certain form, what is its optimal meaning? OT syntax can thus be seen as taking the point of view of the speaker, and OT semantics as taking the point of view of the hearer. By taking the point of view of the hearer, OT semantics assumes a surface form as the input, and optimizes over a set of candidate interpretations of this surface form. Violable constraints on interpretation determine which candidate interpretation is the optimal, or preferred, interpretation of this surface form and hence yields the output to the optimization process.

One constraint that seems to play an important part in interpretation is a pragmatic constraint that favors anaphorization of text. We adopt Williams' (1997) formulation of this constraint:

(5) DOAP: Don't Overlook Anaphoric Possibilities: Opportunities to anaphorize text must be seized.

This principle accounts for the fact that there is a general preference to interpret linguistic elements as anaphors, relating them to the previous discourse. DOAP can easily be overruled, however. Krahmer and van Deemter (1997) observe that the definite NP *the doctor* is not readily interpreted as anaphoric to the preceding NP *a doctor* in (6):

(6) Often when I talk to a doctor, the doctor disagrees with him.

According to Krahmer and van Deemter, the anaphoric interpretation is ruled out here because of the implausiblity of the resulting reading. However, if that were the case, *the doctor* would not be interpreted as anaphoric in (7) either.

(7) Often when I talk to a doctor, the doctor disagrees with himself.

But, in fact, the anaphoric reading is the preferred reading in (7). Rather, what seems to be going on in (6) is a conflict between the pragmatic constraint DOAP and another constraint on interpretation:

(8) PRINCIPLE B: If two arguments of the same semantic relation are not marked as being identical, interpret them as being distinct.

The constraint PRINCIPLE B in (8) is, in fact, the violable counterpart of the well-known Principle B of the Binding Theory (cf. Farmer & Harnish, 1987; cf. Reinhart & Reuland, 1993). Whereas DOAP and PRINCIPLE B can both be satisfied in (7), DOAP is violated in (6) in order to satisfy PRINCIPLE B. Hence, PRINCIPLE B must be ranked higher than DOAP. The interaction between DOAP and PRINCIPLE B in the interpretation of (6) and (7) is illus-

trated in the Tableaux (7) and (8). In Tableau (7), the input is the sentence in
(6). The candidate outputs are possible interpretations for the NPs *a doctor*,
the doctor and *him*. Note that, by focusing on the interpretations of these
NPs only, we abstract away from other interpretational issues and the constraints pertaining to these issues.

TABLEAU 7
NP interpretation (1)

Input: Sentence (6)	PRINCIPLE B	DOAP
☞ a doctor$_1$ – the doctor$_1$ – him$_2$		*
☞ a doctor$_1$ – the doctor$_2$ – him$_1$		*
a doctor$_1$ – the doctor$_1$ – him$_1$	*!	
a doctor$_1$ – the doctor$_2$ – him$_2$	*!	*
a doctor$_1$ – the doctor$_2$ – him$_3$		**!

In Tableau (8), the input is the sentence in (7). The candidate outputs are
possible interpretations for the NPs *a doctor*, *the doctor* and *himself*.

TABLEAU 8
NP interpretation (2)

Input: Sentence (7)	PRINCIPLE B	DOAP
a doctor$_1$ – the doctor$_1$ – himself$_2$		*!
a doctor$_1$ – the doctor$_2$ – himself$_1$		*!
☞ a doctor$_1$ – the doctor$_1$ – himself$_1$		
a doctor$_1$ – the doctor$_2$ – himself$_2$		*!
a doctor$_1$ – the doctor$_2$ – himself$_3$		*!*

According to Tableau 7, two optimal interpretations are obtained for (6).
These two interpretations satisfy the stronger PRINCIPLE B while violating
the weaker DOAP only once. They are obtained when either *the doctor* or
him is coreferential with *a doctor*. For (7), we obtain only one optimal interpretation, as can be seen in Tableau 8. Here, the winning candidate satisfies
both PRINCIPLE B and DOAP. According to this interpretation, *a doctor*, *the
doctor* and *himself* all refer to the same discourse entity.

This example illustrates how OT might be applied to the domain of interpretation. The interpretation of NPs seems to depend on the interaction
among violable constraints. Notably, these constraints on interpretation involve different types of linguistic knowledge: pragmatic knowledge, syntactic knowledge, semantic knowledge, etcetera. Nothing in the architecture of

OT requires constraint interaction to be modular. As we will see in later chapters, optimization in the domain of interpretation is characterized by truly **cross-modular constraint interaction**.

At this point, nothing was said yet about cross-linguistic differences with respect to interpretation. The main motivation for applying OT to the domain of interpretation has been in its ability to account for cross-modular constraint interaction and the interaction between linguistic knowledge and general world knowledge, rather than in its predictions with respect to cross-linguistic variation. Unfortunately, cross-linguistic variation in the domain of interpretation is still an empirically poorly investigated phenomenon. In this book, cross-linguistic differences will only play a minor role. Focusing on a few languages, we will present language-internal evidence showing the advantages of an OT perspective on semantic and pragmatic issues. This evidence not only involves the interaction among linguistic modules and the interaction between linguistic knowledge, contextual information, and world knowledge, but also the dependence of meanings on forms and *vice versa*.

1.6 Bidirectional Optimization

In the previous sections, OT syntax was presented as taking the point of view of the speaker, and OT semantics as taking the point of view of the hearer. This **one-dimensional view on optimization** is the standard approach in current OT syntax, and was also assumed in some of the earlier applications of OT to the domain of interpretation (Hendriks & de Hoop, 2001; de Hoop & de Swart, 2000). To model both speakers and hearers, the input-output relation formalized by OT syntax must be the inverse of the input-output relation formalized by OT semantics. In general, what we produce we are able to understand adequately and what we understand we are able to produce adequately. However, simply combining OT syntax with OT semantics does not yield a model that assigns a consistent relation between forms and meanings, as was pointed out by Beaver and Lee (2004). That is, under certain choices for the constraints, if you start out with a meaning and apply the OT syntactic constraints to arrive at a certain form, and then apply OT semantic constraints, you may not get back to the original meaning. One way to avoid these mismatches between form and meaning is by adopting a bidirectional approach to optimization.

According to Blutner (2000), the hearer perspective and the speaker perspective cannot be taken in isolation from each other. Blutner argues in favor of **bidirectional optimization**, where speaker's and hearer's optimization are carried out simultaneously. In Blutner's (2000) version of bidirectional OT, a form-meaning pair <f,m> is called **super-optimal** if and only if there is no other super-optimal pair <f',m> such that <f',m> ≺ <f,m>, and there is no other super-optimal pair <f,m'> such that <f,m'> ≺ <f,m> (≺ is an ordering relation which can be read as 'being less costly, being more harmonic, being more economical'). Under this view, form-meaning pairs that compete in one direction of optimization are constrained by the outcomes of the other direction, and vice versa. In principle, two types of super-optimal form-meaning pairs can be distinguished: the ones consisting of an unmarked form and an unmarked meaning, and the ones consisting of a marked form and a marked meaning. Both are super-optimal, because there are no alternative super-optimal pairs such that either the form is more economical with respect to that same meaning, or the meaning is more adequate with respect to that same form. For example, consider the following sentences, originally due to Grice:

(9) Mrs. T produced a series of sounds closely resembling the score of 'Home Sweet Home'.

(10) Mrs. T sang 'Home Sweet Home'.

The long and unusual form in (9) is used to convey that there is something special with the singing, for example that it is not particularly nice. In bidirectional OT, this can be explained straightforwardly. The long form is rejected for the standard meaning. To convey the standard meaning we have a simpler and more usual form, namely the sentence in (10). Likewise, the simple form in (10) is rejected for the non-standard meaning because the simple form is already associated with the standard meaning. The result is that the simple form is associated with the simple meaning, and the long and unusual form is associated with the non-standard meaning. Thus, Blutner's bidirectional OT accounts for the generalization that marked forms tend to be used for marked meanings and unmarked forms for unmarked meanings, a phenomenon which is sometimes referred to as **iconicity**. Blutner's approach also captures cases of **blocking**: a form does not exist because an alternative form already does. This phenomenon of blocking shows that we also must take into consideration what else the speaker could have said.

As will be discussed in more detail in Chapter 4, the concept of bidirectional optimization also provides a formalization of **Grice's maximes of conversation** (Grice, 1975). In particular, bidirectional optimization models the competing forces of minimizing the speaker's efforts and minimizing the hearer's efforts. Minimization of the speaker's efforts corresponds to the second part of Grice's maxim of quantity: *do not make your contribution more informative than is required*. It also corresponds to Grice's maxim of relation and possibly Grice's maxims of manner.

Bidirectional OT seeks to select the most coherent interpretation, by comparing different possible meanings for the same form. This part of bidirectional optimization is much in line with the one-dimensional view on optimality theoretic interpretation mentioned above, which exclusively adopts the hearer perspective. In addition, bidirectional optimization also takes into account the speaker perspective. This results in a minimization of the hearer's efforts, corresponding to the first part of Grice's maxim of quantity: *make your contribution as informative as required*. It acts as a blocking mechanism which blocks all the outputs for which there is a more economical input, by comparing different possible forms that the speaker could have used to communicate the same meaning.

The idea to compare not only different outputs with each other to determine the optimal interpretation, but also take into account different inputs, was already present in Prince and Smolensky's (1993) lexicon optimization. Bidirectional optimization also plays a role in Tesar and Smolensky's (1998) learning algorithm. This learning algorithm will be explained briefly in the next chapter and discussed in more detail in Chapter 5. In phonology, a similar kind of bidirectional optimization has been proposed by Boersma (1998). Boersma argues that sound structures reflect an interaction between the articulatory and perceptual principles of efficient and effective communication. From the speaker perspective, there is a minimization of articulatory effort. From the hearer perspective, there is a minimization of perceptual confusion. This suggests that bidirectional optimization occurs throughout the grammar and is not restricted to interpretation. In the next section, we will speculate on the way the architecture of such a grammar might look like.

1.7 The Architecture of Grammar

Informally speaking, a grammar is a system that relates meanings to forms and forms to meanings. Speakers try to find the optimal form to express a given meaning. Hearers try to find the optimal meaning for a given form. Because the grammar is embedded within the cognitive system, we must not only look at the grammar itself but also at the way it interacts with the rest of the cognitive system. A provisional sketch of the architecture of a bidirectional OT grammar is presented in Figure 2.

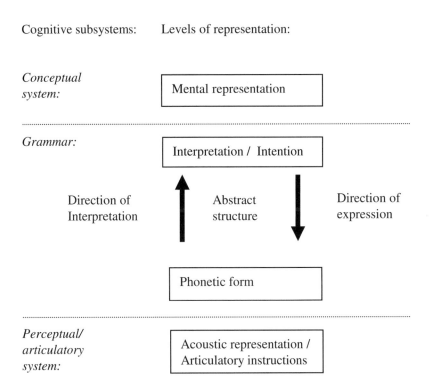

Figure 2 The architecture of the bidirectional OT grammar

As can be seen from Figure 2, at least three cognitive subsystems are involved in language production and language interpretation. The basic idea is that (spoken) language is a way to convey thoughts through sounds. For this reason, language involves the system of grammar (with its linguistic representations), the system of thoughts (with its mental representations) and the system of sound perception and production (with its acoustic representations and motor instructions to the speech organs). The conceptual system and the perceptual and articulatory system are certainly much more complex than is suggested in this figure. However, since we are concerned with the architecture of the grammar mainly, we will not discuss the structure of these non-linguistic systems.

Within the grammar, a distinction is made between two levels of representation. At the one end of the grammar, there is the **level of meaning** (namely: interpretation and intention). We will assume that the meaning of a sentence can be identified with the conditions under which this sentence is true. For example, the sentence *All boys are laughing* is true if the set of boys is a subset of the set of laughing individuals. At the other end of the grammar, there is the **level of form** (to be more specific: phonetic form). For the sentence *All boys are laughing*, this is a phonetic representation of this sentence. The arrows indicate the direction of optimization. Interpretation proceeds from form to meaning. Expression proceeds from meaning to form. Assuming a bidirectional view on optimization, establishing the meaning for a given form involves taking into account both directions of optimization.

In between the levels of meaning and form, the term 'abstract structure' appears in Figure 2. As was already pointed out before, GEN structures the input into an infinite number of output candidates. For example, if the input is a meaning, GEN generates a set of structured forms. Similarly, if the input is a form, GEN generates a set of structured meaning representations. Because candidates are evaluated with respect to this abstract structure, this abstract structure is always part of the output. But this implies that there is no need to postulate a separate level of abstract or underlying structure in between the levels of meaning and form. Such a level of abstract structure is superfluous in bidirectional OT since the necessary abstract structure is already present at one of the other levels. Therefore, no separate level of abstract or underlying structure is distinguished in Figure 2. The proposed grammar only needs to distinguish two levels of representation, namely the level of meaning and the level of form. Abstract structure is introduced by GEN into the candidate set. Of course, this puts the burden of abstract structure completely on GEN. In the rest of this book, we will see whether there is some support for this view or whether it needs to be adjusted.

One might wonder whether it is necessary to distinguish between a grammatical level of phonetic form and a perceptual level of acoustic representation, since both are representational levels of form. Similarly, should we distinguish between a grammatical level of interpretation and a conceptual level of mental representation? Both are representational levels of meaning. The answer is yes. A characteristic of the system of language is that it makes use of **discrete representations**. While speech sounds are non-discrete, their phonological representations are discrete. For example, the distinction between a [b] and a [p] is a gradient one and depends on the voice onset time. However, humans perceive and use these speech sounds in a categorial way. A sound is generally perceived as either a [b] or a [p]. Moreover, when these sounds occur in the context of a word, the resulting meanings are not gradient at all. So if a sound is in between a [b] and a [p] and if this sound precedes the string [ɛt], we do not get a meaning that is in between the meaning of *bet* and the meaning of *pet*. A similar distinction appears to be involved in meaning. Real world objects cannot always be distinguished in a discrete way. For example, the distinction between a cup and a bowl is a gradient one. On the other hand, lexical and sentential meanings seem to be used in a discrete way. To refer to an object which is somewhere in between a cup and a bowl, we do not use a linguistic form which is somewhere in between the linguistic form *cup* and the linguistic form *bowl*, for example *cowl* or *bup*. Rather, we combine discrete linguistic forms and refer to this object by *small bowl*, or *large cup*, or *very large cup*. So in general, the system of grammar seems to be characterized by its discrete nature. This separates it from the conceptual system and the perceptual and articulatory system, which relate nondiscrete structures to discrete structures and vice versa.

Another reason to distinguish two levels of form and two levels of meaning concerns the nature of the output of optimization. As was already put forward, GEN generates **structured representations**. Because optimization can proceed in either direction, both the level of interpretation and the level of phonetic form contain structure. However, linguistic structure is never pronounced. Therefore, there must be a level of form which does not contain any abstract structure and hence is distinct from the level of phonetic form. At this level, the form of an utterance is encoded as a linear sequence of motor instructions to the speech organs. Similarly, at the meaning side linguistic structure does not refer to the real world or to any imaginary world. Hence, linguistic structure does not play a role at the level of mental representation. The two levels of form and the two levels of meaning might truly be two separate levels of representation. Alternatively, the linguistic levels might just be higher-level descriptions of the lower-level properties and computations of the brain, in accordance with Smolensky's views on the relation between the symbolic level of OT and the subsymbolic level of neural computation (see Chapter 6).

In Chapter 3, we show that **contextual information** plays an important role in interpretation. An important question is where this contextual information is located in the architecture in Figure 2. To answer this question, let us look at a concrete example. If we wish to produce a sentence, the linguistic and extralinguistic context determine which discourse entities are more salient than others. Because the most salient discourse entity tends to be used as the subject, context influences the structure of the sentence. So sentence (11) is most easily used in a context where Volkert is the most salient discourse entity, whereas (12) is most easily used in a context where Pim is the most salient discourse entity.

(11) Volkert killed Pim.

(12) Pim was killed (by Volkert).

Because context partly determines which discourse entity occurs in subject position and which discourse entity in object position, context must be part of the input of the optimization process. At the same time, the sentence provides an update of the salience list. If the current subject is not the most salient discourse entity of the preceding context, this subject becomes the most salient discourse entity of the new context. For example, even if Volkert were the most salient discourse entity in the context, we could use sentence (12), with the effect that now Pim becomes the most salient discourse entity. So context should also be part of the output of the optimization process. That is, context interacts with the grammar at all levels of linguistic representation.

In this first chapter, we did not discuss the issue of where the universal OT constraints come from. Most phonologists agree that phonological markedness is ultimately **grounded** in factors outside of the grammatical system (Kager, 1999: 5). In particular, the systems of articulation and perception naturally impose limitations on which sounds and sound sequences should be favored. This would provide an interesting alternative to the hypothesis that all constraints are innate, although phonetic grounding is still lacking for a number of constraints. In a similar fashion, one might argue for the cognitive grounding of certain interpretational markedness constraints. It is not unthinkable that the system of mental representation imposes limitations on which interpretations should be favored. For example, an interpretational constraint such as AVOID CONTRADICTION might be grounded in general cognitive abilities. In general, people do not like pieces of information they receive (be it from a visual or auditive source, or from linguistic knowledge or world knowledge, or a combination) to contradict each other. In these cases, often a decision is forced by treating certain clues as more important than others. However, this is an area which has not yet been investigated.

1.8 Relation to Other Semantic Frameworks

In this section we relate the optimality theoretic framework of semantic interpretation to other semantic theories. Moreover, we substantiate the claim that the unifying framework of OT helps to integrate the advantages of several different semantic theories.

In one way or another, most theories of semantics can be seen as reactions to what is known as the **classical theory of semantics**. The classical theory holds that the meaning of natural language expressions relates to their truth-conditional content. What this means is that the meanings of lexical elements have a definitional structure: they encode necessary and sufficient conditions for determining their extension. The standard example is connected with the concept BACHELOR (where concepts are indicated by small caps) expressing the meaning of *bachelor*. According to the classical theory, we can think of the concept as a complex mental representation that specifies necessary and sufficient conditions for something to be a bachelor. Standardly, it is assumed that the concept BACHELOR is composed of the following set of representations: IS NOT MARRIED, IS MALE, IS AN ADULT. Each of these components is seen as a semantic feature with a given extension. Using the logical operation of conjunction as connecting the semantic components, the interpretation of the complex concept BACHELOR can be determined in accordance with the principle of compositional semantics.

The principle of compositionality is also applied when it comes to calculating the meaning of a complex expression like *Peter is a bachelor* or *Every bachelor likes young ladies*. In this case, the logical operations that create the sentence meaning from the lexical meanings are related to the syntactic term algebra that structures the sentence (typically, the operations of functional application and functional composition play an important role).

The classical approach has numerous advantages, for instance the clarity and stringency of the architecture (capturing the productivity of language and thought), the powerful and tractable theory of categorization it is suggesting, its ability to deal with a variety of semantic phenomena, especially analytic inferences, antonymy, ambiguity, hyponymy, and reference determination. However, there is a long list of serious problems and shortcomings. Besides others, it contains the following issues (for details we have to refer to the literature, e.g. Barsalou et al., 1995; Margolis & Laurence, 1999):

- Plato's problem: there are few, if any, examples of defined concepts.
- The problem of analyticity: Quine's (1951/1980) arguments against analyticity also work against the claim that the meanings of lexical units can be defined in a strict logical sense.
- The symbolic grounding problem: no account is given of how symbolic representations are linked to their referents in the world. Instead, symbols only become linked to the world through the theorists and programmers who create them.

- The problem of fuzziness: categorization admits a certain amount of indeterminacy.
- The problem of centrality or prototypicality: how to accommodate typicality?
- The problem of context: the classical approach does not respect the role of open and hidden indexicality which affects most lexical concepts and calls for a proper treatment of context.

With regard to the last mentioned problem, we have to acknowledge the interest of model-theoretic semantics in a formal treatment of indexical expressions, inspired primarily by the work of Montague (e.g. Montague, 1970). The basic idea was to overcome some fallacies of the traditional truth-functional theories by introducing aspects of context into formal semantics. As a result of these efforts, a **classical theory of context-dependency** originated (Kaplan, 1979).

Within this theory, the connection between meaning and extension/reference is established in two steps. The meaning $\|\alpha\|$ (or the **character**) of an expression α (in a model M) is a two-place function of context (utterance situation) and index (possible world). Applying the character $\|\alpha\|$ to a context c, the intension $\|\alpha\|<c>$ of α in this context results. The intension itself can be understood as a function, which applied to an index w results in the extension $\|\alpha\|<c><w>$.

So-called Kaplan contexts c include a specification of factors characterizing the speech situation, such as the agent c_{ag} (speaker), the audience c_{aud}, the time of utterance c_T, the place of utterance c_p, and a characterization of the reference situation c_w (the world of utterance). It is straightforward that a Kaplan context can be augmented by including further components into the list of contextual elements, which can be used for describing the phenomena of polysemy (cf. Bartsch, 1987) and predicate transfer (Sag, 1981), for instance.

Interestingly, within context-dependent semantics, the principle of compositionality is required to apply to characters. In the case of descriptive expressions, where the characters do not really depend on context, the principle of compositionality can be transferred to the level of intensions. However, compositionality with respect to intensions may be violated when true context-dependencies come into play. As discussed elsewhere (e.g. Blutner, 2002, 2004), this can become a problem if we try to explain the systematic patterns and restrictions found in predicate transfer and polysemy (Nunberg, 1979, 1995).

Many researchers postulate a division of labor between (i) a linguistic system determining the semantic representation of a sentence (grammar including the lexicon) and (ii) a pragmatic system constituting the interpretation of the corresponding utterance in a given setting (contextual information, encyclopedia). In context-dependent semantics this division of labour is reduced to the distinction between characters (meanings) and intensions, which are available in particular contexts. Consequently, the constitution of context is the crucial part of pragmatics.

This analysis contrasts with the view of '**radical pragmatics**' (cf. Cole, 1981). According to this view, the pragmatic system is taken as realizing Grice's (1975) idea of conversational implicature. This implies a completely different picture of the pragmatic system where the constitution of context is an important part, but the architecture of pragmatics is determined by its own principles and maxims. Chapter 4 is devoted to modeling these ideas with the instruments of OT.

So far we were concerned with 'static' conceptions of meaning, where meaning conforms to truth conditions or to functions immediately leading to truth conditions. Starting with Kamp (1981) and Heim (1982) a new conception of meaning was developed which aimed to describe the **change of (discourse) context** that is brought about by uttering a sentence. Whereas Kamp's original paper is clearly based on the tenets of 'radical pragmatics' in realizing a programmatic outline of a cognitively oriented approach to language, much research which falls under the rubric of the 'dynamic turn' is in the spirit of the conservative view of language which radical pragmatics set itself against (for details, cf. Blutner & Zeevat, 2004). While the compositionality assumption underlying the 'dynamic turn' has strengthened the methodology of semantics, it has also led to a mechanistic approach at points where pragmatics and semantics are difficult to keep apart.

One of the main deficiencies of the classical approaches (including classical theories of context-dependency) is their inflexibility and incompetence in dealing with stereotypical information, defaults, nonmonotonicity of inference and prototype effects. The main reason for this deficiency rests in the classical assumption that the involved rules, principles and constraints are inviolable. Overcoming the rigidity of inviolable constraints and accounting for conflict resolution in systems of violable constraints clears the way for a proper analysis of prototypicality and fuzziness, and likewise for overcoming Plato's problem. Optimality Theory can be seen as a general framework that allows us to express these new ideas in a precise and tractable way. In particular, this holds for several ideas that are formulated in theories deviating in crucial aspects from the classical theory.

Some of these ideas conform to **prototype theory**. Prototype theory assumes that most concepts are structured mental representations that encode the properties that objects in their extension tend to possess (an excellent introduction gives Margolis & Laurence, 1999). Thus, the features of a concept are not taken to be necessary as they were in the classical theory, and in some cases some members of the category may be in conflict with one or several of these prototypical features. Probably the most attractive aspect of prototype theory is the treatment of categorization, which helps to overcome Plato's problem. On this model, an instance is taken to be a member of a category just in cases the feature representation of the instance and the feature representation of the category are sufficiently similar.

However, prototype theory does not solve all of the problems classical theory cannot solve. For instance, it does not solve the symbolic grounding problem and it does not solve the problem of context. Furthermore, it introduces new problems: the most famous one is that prototype theory does not have an adequate account of compositionality (e.g. Osherson & Smith, 1981).

Another kind of theories are the so-called **neoclassical theories** (cf. Laurence & Margolis, 1999). They emphasize the commitment of the classical theory to necessary conditions and they add other conditions that express default conditions or conditions that typically apply to the instances of a category (cf. Jackendoff, 1983). Accordingly, neoclassical theories can be seen as providing partial definitions that may be completed by applying default information in a given context. As discussed by Laurence and Margolis (1999), this theory suffers from the **problem of completers**. In short, this problem refers to the following dilemma:

> On the one hand, if the partial definitions are turned into full definitions, then all of the problems that the classical theory faced return. On the other hand, if they are left as partial definitions, then the neoclassical theory is without an account of reference determination. (Laurence & Margolis, 1999: 54).

In our opinion, the problem of completers has to do with a too simplistic picture of the optimization procedure: start from a partial semantic definition and complete it (in an optimal way) to find out the full definition. Let us assume that the partial semantic definitions account for the grammatically relevant structure only, with the consequence that the words *tiger* and *lion* or *melt* and *freeze* have the same partial definitions. In order to solve the problem of completers, we simply have to assume that the initial point of optimization includes more than the mentioned partial semantic representation. For instance, we can assume that it also contains syntactic, lexical, and contextual information, and in some cases it should contain information on the prosodic structure of the utterance as well. OT is intended as a framework that assumes that all kinds of constraints are exploited simultaneously. Hence, the integration of pragmatic and syntactic/semantic information in a system of ranked constraints is proposed to correctly derive the optimal interpretations for natural language inputs.

Taken together, our hope is that the general and unifying framework of OT helps us to integrate the advantages of different semantic theories without taking over all their shortcomings.

1.9 An Overview of the Book

The main hypothesis of this book is that optimization plays a crucial role in communication, just as it has been argued for other domains of cognition. Such a perspective allows for a clear view on the relation between knowledge of grammar versus the use of this grammar since the use of the grammar is assumed to reflect the knowledge of the grammar directly. Differences between production and comprehension result from the different direction of optimization (from meaning to form or from form to meaning). Whereas a speaker optimizes syntactic structure with respect to a semantic input (the speaker's 'thought' or intention), a hearer optimizes the interpretation of a certain utterance in a certain context. But we need to go one step further. That is, the speaker needs to verify whether the hearer will indeed arrive at the intended interpretation on the basis of the form she chooses. Similarly, the hearer needs to verify on the basis of the interpretation she gets whether she would have used the same given form to express that interpretation when she would have been the speaker. Therefore, the determination of an optimal expression or an optimal interpretation is always dependent on the other direction of optimization as well. In this first chapter, the basic concepts of Optimality Theory were introduced. In the remainder of this book we argue that the process of optimization in communication cannot be unidirectional, since the ultimate goal of an agent involved in communication is to understand correctly and to be understood correctly. A prime aim of this book is to show that optimal communication is bidirectional.

A proper treatment of interpretation involves taking into account both the perspective of the hearer and the perspective of the speaker. This is done by adopting a bidirectional Optimality Theoretic approach to interpretation. In **Chapter 2**, it is shown that the syntactic requirement of recoverability on deletion automatically follows from such a bidirectional approach to interpretation. In **Chapter 3**, it is shown that problems with the semantic principle of compositionality can be solved by adopting a weakened version of compositionality. This weakened version of compositionality also conforms to a bidirectional approach to interpretation. Bidirectional Optimality Theory can be characterized in game-theoretical terms. Therefore, the framework has a strong formal background. Nevertheless, pragmatic concepts such as Grice's conversational maxims can be reinterpreted quite straight-forwardly within this framework. This is the topic of **Chapter 4**. Because a bidirectional perspective on optimization requires a different view on learn-ing, an entire chapter (**Chapter 5**) is devoted to this issue. Historically, Op-timality Theory is rooted in connectionism, which does not assume a strict distinction between representation and processing. In the final chapter of the book (**Chapter 6**), therefore, connections are explored between bidirec-tional Optimality Theory and connectionist computation.

2

Recoverability

2.1 Introduction

In this chapter we demonstrate how the form of a sentence arises as the result of competing forces. In particular, we will look at syntactic movement and deletion. Our starting point is the idea that a linguistic form, such as a sentence, can be viewed as a carrier of information. Because sentences are finite and therefore can encode only a limited amount of information, choices have to be made with respect to the information that is encoded and the way this information is encoded. The form of the sentence can thus be considered the result of different forces competing with each other for the limited coding possibilities offered by the sentence. Not every piece of information will eventually be encoded in the structure of the sentence. Neither will it be the case that each encoded piece of information individually is encoded in the best possible way. However, the way all these pieces of information together are encoded in the sentence is the best possible, or optimal, way to encode this specific combination of information. Hence, the syntactic structure of a sentence is the outcome of a process of optimization with respect to competing forces.

This chapter is organized as follows. In Section 2.2, Ackema and Neeleman's OT analysis of movement in questions is presented. Section 2.3 discusses Kennedy's OT analysis of deletion in comparative constructions. Several problems are shown to arise with respect to the recoverability of deleted material when adopting a productive optimization approach. These will be discussed in Section 2.4. Here, it is argued that a bidirectional approach to sentence production is required to solve these problems.

2.2 Movement

In English, sentences tend to display the basic word order subject-verb-object. This basic pattern is illustrated in (1).

(1)   Kim has seen a unicorn.

The subject *Kim* precedes the finite verb *has*, which precedes the direct object *a unicorn*. Now suppose we do not know what Kim has seen. We could then ask the following question:

(2)   What has Kim seen?

Interestingly, here it is the direct object *what* that comes first. This shows that there is an even greater force than the force that determines **canonical word order**. This greater force requires WH-expressions such as *what* to appear in sentence initial position. As shown in Ackema and Neeleman (1998), these data can be explained very elegantly by the competition among violable constraints in an OT framework. The exposition in this section therefore borrows heavily from their analysis.

Let us call the force, or constraint, that favors the canonical position for each argument in the sentence STAY (cf. Grimshaw, 1997).

(3)   STAY: Do not move.

This constraint expresses the fact that words do not like to be moved around in the sentence. Rather, they prefer to appear in the position given by the basic word order of the sentence. Important to note here is that the basic word order results from other constraints, which we will not discuss here. The constraint STAY actually is a very general constraint with respect to structural economy, expressing the fact that movement is costly. In contrast to Grimshaw (1997), Ackema and Neeleman interpret STAY as a constraint that can be violated several times: the longer the path between the moved item and its original position in the derivation, the more violations of STAY result. The length of the path is measured in terms of nodes in the path. For the sake of simplicity, however, we will assume here that movement of a subject induces one violation of STAY, movement of the finite verb two violations, and movement of an object three violations.

The other force playing a role in question formation can be modeled by two constraints that are particular to question formation:

(4)   Q-SCOPE: A WH-expression must take scope over its clause.

Q-MARKING: A question must be Q-marked.

These two constraints promote the encoding of essential aspects of the meaning of questions in the structure of a sentence.

The constraint Q-SCOPE requires a WH-expression, which carries the feature [+Q], to have an entire proposition in its scope. Because the constraints discussed here are constraints with respect to the overt form of the sentence, they all apply at surface structure. Therefore, Q-SCOPE requires WH-expressions to overtly appear in a position c-commanding the clause expressing the proposition. This constraint thus promotes **overt movement** of the WH-expression to the highest position in the sentence: the specifier position of CP.

The other constraint that is particular to question formation is Q-MARKING. This constraint expresses the requirement that a question must carry a feature marking it for questionhood. Because properties are usually marked by a head on its complement, this constraint requires the clause to be the complement of a [+Q] head. This is the case only if, in addition to movement of the WH-expression to the specifier position of CP, the finite verb moves to C. These two instances of movement are depicted in Figure 1.

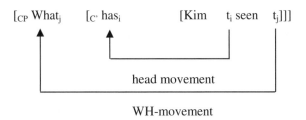

Figure 1 Movement in questions

To see that only the combination of WH-movement and verb movement allows for the clause to be Q-marked, let us look at the phenomenon of Q-marking in somewhat more detail. A lexical property of WH-expressions is that they carry the feature [+Q]. Therefore, the presence of a WH-expression introduces the feature [+Q] into the sentence. By the general mechanism of specifier-head agreement, a WH-expression in specifier position will transfer its feature [+Q] to a finite verb in C-position. Now this head is capable of Q-marking its complement clause through the mechanism of head-complement marking. Clearly, if there is no verb in C-position, the clause will not be Q-marked. Under this analysis, therefore, the function of movement of the verb to C is to make it possible to transfer the feature [+Q] from the WH-expression to its clause employing standard mechanisms of the grammar such as specifier-head agreement and head-complement marking.

$$[_{CP} \quad What_j \quad [_{C'} \quad has_i \quad \quad [Kim \quad t_i \, seen \quad t_j]]]$$

[+Q]	----▶	[+Q]	----▶	[+Q]
	spec-head-agreement		head-complement-marking	

Figure 2 Q-marking

Because this is the only way for the clause to be Q-marked, Q-MARKING forces movement of the WH-expression as well as of the finite verb.

Now let us look at the way these three constraints interact. Whereas the constraint STAY requires elements to stay in their canonical position, the other two constraints force movement. Therefore, these constraints are highly conflicting. If a WH-expression is not base-generated in a position c-commanding the clause, it must violate at least one of these constraints. There is no way a WH-expression in that position can satisfy all three constraints at the same time. Depending on the relative strengths of the constraints, the WH-expression will remain in its base-generated position or move to a scope position. Similarly, the finite verb will either remain in its base-generated position or move to C to be able to Q-mark the clause.

The interaction between these three constraints explains the formation of **simple questions** in English. In English, Q-MARKING must be ranked above STAY, or we would never have WH-movement in English. Q-SCOPE is ordered lowest. As the input, we assume a predicate-argument structure with some additional information, for example {see(x,y), x = Kim, y = what, tense = perfect} (see Section 1.5 of Chapter 1). From this input, a set of candidates is generated. The relevant candidates are the four possibilities obtained by moving or not moving the WH-expression and moving or not moving the finite verb. Actually, in principle an infinite number of candidates are possible and many more constraints apply, but we omit candidates and constraints that are not relevant to the present discussion.

TABLEAU 1
Simple questions in English

Input: {see(x,y), x = Kim, y = what, tense = perfect}	Q-MARKING	STAY	Q-SCOPE
☞ What$_j$ has$_i$ [Kim t$_i$ seen t$_j$]		*****	
What$_j$ [Kim has seen t$_j$]	*!	***	
Has$_i$ [Kim t$_i$ seen what]	*!	**	*
[Kim has seen what]	*!		*

The first candidate is obtained by moving both the WH-expression and the finite verb. In the second candidate, only WH-movement has applied. The finite verb remains in situ. The third candidate is obtained by moving only the finite verb. In the fourth candidate, no movement at all occurred. Because the fourth candidate is the only candidate that does not involve any movement, this is the only candidate to satisfy the constraint STAY. The constraint Q-SCOPE is satisfied by the two candidates in which the WH-expression is moved to a position where it c-commands its clause, that is, by the first and the second candidate. The third constraint, Q-MARKING, can only be satisfied by moving both the WH-expression and the finite verb. Therefore, the first candidate is the only candidate to satisfy this constraint. Since Q-MARKING is ranked highest, the first candidate is the optimal candidate with respect to these three ranked constraints. So if Q-MARKING is ranked above STAY as well as Q-SCOPE, we obtain the correct results for English. In English, both the WH-expression and the finite verb must be moved. Note that the relative ranking of STAY and Q-SCOPE is not important for this example because there is only one candidate that satisfies Q-MARKING.

A crucial assumption underlying this line of reasoning is the assumption that the constraints are ordered by **strict domination**. No number of violations of the lower ranked constraint STAY can overpower a single violation of the higher ranked constraint Q-MARKING. This is assumed to be a fundamental property of OT (see also Chapter 1).

As this example shows, OT syntax takes a **speaker perspective**. It starts with a representation of the meaning as its input. From this input, the generator GEN generates an infinite set of competing candidate structures. Potentially conflicting constraints apply to this set of candidates and select the structural representation, often termed **structural description**, that best satisfies these constraints. A structural description not only includes the overt structure directly accessible to the hearer, but also the hidden structure necessary for the evaluation of candidates. In our example, hidden structure includes the phrasal structure of the sentence and the original positions of the moved expressions, indicated by *t*. The structural description that best satisfies the constraints yields the output form which is pronounced.

From this example, it appears as if Q-MARKING alone suffices to explain the data. Because the three suboptimal candidates all violate this constraint, their behavior with respect to the other two lower ranked constraints is not relevant anymore for this particular example. However, if we look at more complex examples, the other constraints become important. Consider an example of a **multiple question**, in which we have two WH-expressions:

(5)   Who has seen what?

Because Q-MARKING is ranked highest, the finite verb and at least one WH-expression must move in order to allow for Q-marking of its clause. The following OT-tableau shows what happens to the other WH-expression in languages such as English. The input to optimization is the representation $\{see(x,y), x = who, y = what, tense = perfect\}$.

TABLEAU 2
Multiple questions in English

Input: $\{see(x,y), x = who, y = what, tense = perfect\}$	Q-MARKING	STAY	Q-SCOPE
Who$_i$ what$_k$ has$_j$ [t$_i$ t$_j$ seen t$_k$]		****!**	
☞ Who$_i$ has$_j$ [t$_i$ t$_j$ seen what]		***	*
Who$_i$ what$_k$ [t$_i$ has seen t$_k$]	*!	****	
What$_k$ has$_j$ [who t$_j$ seen t$_k$]		****!*	*
Who$_i$ [t$_i$ has seen what]	*!	*	*
Has$_j$ [who t$_j$ seen what]	*!	**	**
What$_k$ [who has seen t$_k$]	*!	***	*
[Who has seen what]	*!		**

Here, we have eight options, obtained by moving or not moving the WH-subject, moving or not moving the finite verb, and moving or not moving the WH-object. Although some of the candidates result in the same overt form, for example the second, fifth and eighth candidate, their evaluation with respect to the constraints differs because they have different structural descriptions.

Because three candidates satisfy Q-MARKING, here the lower ranked constraints become important. If STAY were ranked below Q-SCOPE, the second WH-expression would be predicted to move out of the clause. However, this is not the case for English. In English, the second WH-expression remains in situ. This follows if STAY is ranked higher than Q-SCOPE. This example therefore yields a nice illustration of the property of OT that the effects of lower ranked constraints become visible if higher ranked constraints are satisfied by more than one candidate. In fact, the lower ranked constraint STAY has two effects on the structure of multiple questions in English: it accounts for the fact that all WH-expressions but one remain in situ, and it accounts for the fact that the WH-expression that is moved is the one that makes the shortest possible move and thus violates STAY the fewest number of times. This explains why moving the WH-subject *who* is preferred to moving the WH-object *what*.

So the interaction among three violable constraints, Q-MARKING, STAY, and Q-SCOPE, explains the formation of simple as well as multiple questions in English. In particular, it provides an account of when WH-expressions must move and when they must stay in situ, and why this is so. Moreover, as Ackema and Neeleman (1998) show, all six possible rankings of these three constraints yield existing languages.

2.3 Deletion

In the previous section, we discussed the forces driving syntactic movement. Another phenomenon which has a clear effect on the surface form of sentences is deletion. Deletion is the omission of words or phrases from the sentence without affecting the interpretation of the sentence. Although most instances of deletion are thought to be optional, a few types of deletion are claimed to be obligatory. In this section, we will look at a particular type of obligatory deletion, namely **comparative deletion** (CD). We will consider the possibility of this type of deletion in two comparative constructions: comparative deletion constructions (CD constructions) and comparative subdeletion constructions (CSD constructions) (cf. Bresnan, 1973). The OT analysis of CD presented in this is taken from Kennedy (2002).

CD is illustrated in (6). CD constructions compare two quantities of the same sort (e.g. numbers of scoring titles, degrees of length, degrees of carefulness).

(6) *Comparative deletion (CD) constructions*

    a. Michael Jordan has more scoring titles than Dennis Rodman has.
    b. The shapes seem to be longer than they are.
    c. My sister drives as carefully as I drive.

CSD is illustrated in (7). CSD constructions compare two quantities of different sorts (e.g. number of scoring titles vs. number of tattoos).

(7) *Comparative subdeletion (CSD) constructions*

    a. Michael Jordan has more scoring titles than Dennis Rodman has tattoos.
    b. The shapes seem to be longer than they are thick.
    c. My sister drives as carefully as I drive carelessly.

CD constructions differ syntactically from CSD constructions in that the compared constituent in the complement-clause of *than* or *as* (henceforth, the *than*-clause) is omitted in CD constructions. In fact, the compared constituent in the *than*-clause is not even allowed to be present, if it is identical to the head of the comparative. If it is present, the result is an unacceptable sentence:

(8)   a. Michael Jordan has more scoring titles than Dennis Rodman has (*scoring titles).
    b. The shapes seem to be longer than they are (*long).
    c. My sister drives as carefully as I drive (*carefully).

Because the verb *has* selects a direct object, a clause such as *Dennis Rodman has* in the CD construction in (6a) in principle is an incomplete clause. However, it is generally assumed that this clause is base-generated as a complete clause, with a compared constituent which is identical to the head of the comparative occurring in the position of the direct object, as in (8a). Thus the selection restrictions of the verb are satisfied. Because the resulting sentence is unacceptable, the compared constituent must be obligatorily removed (through **obligatory deletion** or obligatory movement followed by deletion) from the *than*-clause.

    CD constructions and CSD constructions are highly similar in many respects. For example, they have essentially the same interpretation. In addition, they both require a gap, they both allow for embedding of the gap in contexts from which WH-movement is also allowed, and they are both ill-formed when the gap is embedded in an island for extraction (see Kennedy, 2002, for an exhaustive discussion of these and other similarities). This suggests that CD and CSD should be treated uniformly.

However, a number of syntactic distinctions have been discovered between the two constructions that call into question a uniform treatment (see, e.g. Grimshaw, 1987). For example, CD licences so-called parasitic gaps, whereas CSD does not:

(9) I threw away more books than I kept without reading *e*.

(10) *I threw away more books than I kept magazines without reading *e*.

Here, *e* denotes the parasitic gap. Parasitic gaps are called this way because they are dependent on the presence of another gap. In other words, they require the presence of another gap in the sentence to be felicitous. In particular, as has been observed by Engdahl (1983), parasitic gaps are dependent on traces left behind by overt movement:

(11) a. [Which articles]$_i$ did John file t_i without reading *e*?
      b. *John filed a bunch of articles without reading *e*.

In (11a), the parasitic gap is licensed by the trace left behind by moving *which articles*, whereas in (11b), no movement has taken place and hence no trace is present to license the parasitic gap. As a result, (11b) is unacceptable. The potential for parasitic gaps might thus be viewed as a test for overt movement. The difference in acceptability between (9) and (10) suggests that CD involves overt movement, whereas CSD does not. In addition to the observed difference between CD and CSD with respect to the ability to license a parasitic gap, Kennedy notes a number of other differences between CD and CSD which support the view that the two constructions should receive a distinct analysis.

But if CD constructions and CSD constructions should in fact receive a distinct analysis, how can we account for the observed similarities in interpretation? Alternatively, if CD constructions and CSD constructions should receive a uniform treatment, how can we account for the observed syntactic differences between these constructions? According to Kennedy (2002), the pattern of similarities and contrasts between CD and CSD can be accounted for through the interaction among violable constraints in an Optimality Theoretic framework. Under his account, the same constraints play a role in both constructions. However, their effects differ because the input to the optimization process differs. Recall that CD constructions compare quantities of the same sort, whereas CSD constructions compare quantities of different sorts.

Kennedy proposes to account for CD and CSD using the following four constraints:

(12) STAY: Do not move.
DELETE: Do not pronounce.
C-SCOPE: A compared constituent must take scope over its clause.
RECOVERABILITY: A deleted constituent must be grammatically identical to some other recoverable constituent.

The first constraint is the constraint STAY already familiar from Section 2.2. The second constraint, DELETE, is necessary to allow for the possibility of deletion. Like STAY, this constraint is a general constraint with respect to structural economy. Whereas STAY expresses the fact that movement is costly, this constraint expresses the fact that pronouncing words is costly. A third constraint that Kennedy argues to play a role in comparatives is C-SCOPE. This constraint (which is formulated slightly differently in Kennedy, 2002) resembles the constraint Q-SCOPE that was discussed in the previous section.[1] Both constraints are specific instantiations of the more general constraint requiring operators to occupy a scope taking position.

In addition to these three purely syntactic constraints, Kennedy (2002: 584) introduces the constraint RECOVERABILITY (see also Pesetsky, 1998).[2] According to this constraint, deletion is possible only if the deleted constituent is recoverable. A deleted constituent is recoverable if it is grammatically identical to some other constituent. Kennedy (2002: 589) suggests that 'there is reason to believe that there is in fact an identity relation that holds between the head of the comparative and the copy of the compared constituent in SpecCP'. Although he does not provide an explicit account of this identity relation, Kennedy assumes this identity relation to be the same relation that holds between the head of a relative clause and a moved internal

---

[1] Kennedy formulates C-Scope as follows: 'The compared constituent must occupy the specifier of the complement of than/as' (Kennedy, 2002: 585).

[2] The exact formulation of Kennedy's constraint RECOVERABILITY is: 'For any constituent α, if $\{_{\alpha \ldots}\}$, then there is a constituent $\beta \neq \alpha$ such that β is recoverable and $ID(\alpha,\beta)$, where ID is a grammatical identity relation' (Kennedy, 2002: 584). Pesetsky (1998: 342) formulates his constraint as follows: 'A syntactic unit with semantic content must be pronounced unless it has a sufficiently local antecedent'.

head. Because of this identity relation between a compared constituent in the specifier position of the *than*-clause (SpecCP) and the head of the comparative construction, deletion of a compared constituent is recoverable if this constituent has moved to SpecCP.

The constraint ranking needed to derive the optimal surface form for CD constructions and CSD constructions in English is the following:

(13) RECOVERABILITY » DELETE » STAY » C-SCOPE

Kennedy assumes this ranking to hold at the level of Phonetic Form. To arrive at the correct interpretations for these constructions, Kennedy assumes a different ranking to hold at the level of Logical Form. We will discuss this aspect of Kennedy's analysis in the next section. The effect of the ranking in (13) is that 'deletion is good and overt movement is bad, but it's better to delete than to avoid overt movement' (Kennedy, 2002: 583). Furthermore, deletion is only allowed if the deleted material can be recovered. The situation is essentially the same as with question formation. Whereas STAY prohibits movement, C-SCOPE forces movement, thus giving rise to a conflict between different requirements on the form of the sentence. In addition, the combination of DELETE and RECOVERABILITY forces movement of the compared constituent to the specifier position of CP, because only in this position deletion is licensed.

To see that this ordering of constraints yields the correct results for the two constructions under consideration, consider again sentence (6a), repeated below as (14).

(14) Michael Jordan has more scoring titles than Dennis Rodman has.

In the next section, we will discuss the interpretation of comparatives in more detail. For the moment, however, assume that the input to optimization is a meaning representation that can be paraphrased as: the number of scoring titles Michael Jordan has exceeds the number of scoring titles Dennis Rodman has. Among the candidates to be considered for the *than*-clause of this comparative construction are the following:

(15)   a. than [$_{CP}$ Dennis Rodman has [$_{DP}$ scoring titles]]
       b. than [$_{CP}$ Dennis Rodman has [$_{DP}$ scoring titles]]
       c. than [$_{CP}$ [$_{DP}$ scoring titles]$_i$ Dennis Rodman has t$_i$]
       d. than [$_{CP}$ [$_{DP}$ scoring titles]$_i$ Dennis Rodman has t$_i$]

In (15a), no movement or deletion has occurred. In (15b), no movement has occurred either, but the compared constituent is deleted. In (15c), the compared constituent is moved to SpecCP, but is not deleted. In (15d), finally, the compared constituent is moved to SpecCP, followed by deletion.

TABLEAU 3
Comparative deletion (CD) constructions

Input: quantities of the same sort	RECOVER-ABILITY	DELETE	STAY	C-SCOPE
Sentence (15a)		*!		*
Sentence (15b)	*!			*
Sentence (15c)		*!	*	
☞ Sentence (15d)			*	

In all but one candidate, RECOVERABILITY is satisfied. In (15a) and (15c), this constraint is satisfied vacuously because no deletion has taken place. In (15d), RECOVERABILITY is satisfied because an identity relation holds between the moved compared constituent in SpecCP and the head of the comparative. In (15b), on the other hand, RECOVERABILITY is violated because direct objects cannot be deleted in situ. This is shown by the unacceptability of (16) (see Section 2.4 for a more detailed discussion of this issue).

(16) *Kim knows an astronomer who married [~~DP an astronomer~~].

So (15b) is the only candidate which violates RECOVERABILITY. Constraint DELETE is actually violated by all candidates because all candidates still contain material that must be pronounced. For the sake of simplicity, however, only overt occurrences of the DP *scoring titles* are counted as a violation of DELETE in this tableau. Constraint STAY is violated by candidates (15c) and (15d) because in these sentences the compared constituent is moved to SpecCP. Constraint C-SCOPE is violated by candidates (15a) and (15b) because no compared constituent occupies SpecCP. Thus, the optimal candidate is the candidate in which the compared constituent moves to SpecCP, followed by deletion.

Now let us turn to CSD. Consider again (7a), repeated below as (17).

(17) Michael Jordan has more scoring titles than Dennis Rodman has tattoos.

Let us assume the input to optimization is a meaning representation that can be paraphrased as: the number of scoring titles Michael Jordan has exceeds the number of tattoos Dennis Rodman has. Relevant candidates for the *than*-clause of this sentence are listed below.

(18) a. than [$_{CP}$ Dennis Rodman has [$_{DP}$ tattoos]]
    b. than [$_{CP}$ Dennis Rodman has [$_{DP}$ ~~tattoos~~]]
    c. than [$_{CP}$ [$_{DP}$ tattoos]$_i$ Dennis Rodman has t$_i$]
    d. than [$_{CP}$ [$_{DP}$ ~~tattoos~~]$_i$ Dennis Rodman has t$_i$]

The behavior of these candidates with respect to the four constraints is represented in Tableau 4.

TABLEAU 4
Comparative subdeletion (CSD) constructions

Input: quantities of a different sort	RECOVER-ABILITY	DELETE	STAY	C-SCOPE
☞ Sentence (18a)		*		*
Sentence (18b)	*!			*
Sentence (18c)		*	*!	
Sentence (18d)	*!		*	

In CSD constructions, RECOVERABILITY is not only violated by deletion of the compared constituent in situ, as in (15b), but also by deletion of the moved compared constituent. This is so because the compared constituent *tattoos* is not identical to the head of the comparative construction, *scoring titles*. Because the two remaining candidates both violate DELETE, the lower ranked constraint STAY emerges as the crucial factor when evaluating candidate outputs. Therefore, the optimal candidate is one in which the compared constituent remains in situ. Here we again see a pattern that is quite common in OT: a lower ranked constraint becomes crucial when all relevant candidates equally violate some higher ranked constraints. In OT, this phenomenon is referred to by the term '**emergence of the unmarked**'. Another fundamental property of OT shown here is that violation of the same constraint can result in unacceptability in one case but is allowed in another case. For example, violation of DELETE results in unacceptability in (15a) and (15c) but is not fatal in (18a).

As was shown in this section, only a few constraints on surface forms are needed to explain why we get movement and deletion whenever the compared constituent is identical to the head (CD), but neither movement nor deletion when the head and the compared constituent are not identical (CSD). Using the same set of constraints, syntactic differences between CD constructions and CSD constructions were shown to follow from differences in the input. Because the input for CD constructions and CSD constructions differs slightly, the competing candidates also differ. This results in a different behavior with respect to the constraint RECOVERABILITY.

2.4 Interpreting Comparatives

In this section, we will discuss a number of problems with Kennedy's analysis of comparative formation. As will be argued, Kennedy's analysis suffers from two problems if we consider its consequences within an OT framework: (i) It requires assuming two separate grammars for one language, and (ii) it blurs the distinction between form and meaning. As we will show in this section, these problems can be solved by adopting a bidirectional approach to sentence production.

In the previous section, CD constructions and CSD constructions were argued to differ with respect to certain syntactic properties but to resemble each other with respect to their interpretation. An account was presented of the syntactic differences between CD constructions and CSD constructions. To be able to also account for the similar interpretations of CD constructions and CSD constructions, Kennedy (2002) argues that optimization actually takes place at two different levels of representation. Optimization with respect to the surface form of the sentence takes place at Phonetic Form (PF), whereas optimization with respect to the underlying form of the sentence takes place at Logical Form (LF). Because, according to Kennedy, these two processes of optimization may involve a different ranking of constraints, it is explained why CD constructions and CSD constructions behave differently with respect to their surface form but behave similarly with respect to their interpretation.

(19) a. Constraint ranking at PF (Kennedy, 2002):
    STAY » C-SCOPE
b. Constraint ranking at LF (Kennedy, 2002):
    C-SCOPE » STAY

Ranking of STAY above C-SCOPE at PF has as a result that the compared constituent in a CSD construction prefers to remain in situ rather than overtly move to SpecCP, in contrast to the compared constituent in a CD construction. In the tableaux in the previous section, this ranking was used to determine the optimal form for the two comparative constructions. Ranking of C-SCOPE above STAY at LF has as a result that in both types of comparatives the compared constituent covertly moves to SpecCP. This accounts for the similar interpretations of the two constructions. However, to account for the similar interpretations of CD constructions and CSD constructions there is no need to assume that there are two levels of representation at which the form of the sentence is optimized. In fact, assuming two independent processes of optimization, each with their own constraint ranking, is highly undesirable. Because different constraint rankings actually represent different grammars, it would imply that two separate grammars are required for one language.

In OT, a distinction can be made between productive optimization and interpretive optimization. In productive optimization, different structural descriptions for a given meaning compete:

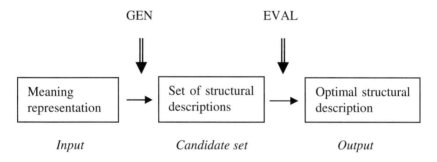

Figure 3 Productive optimization

In interpretive optimization, different semantic representations for a given sentence compete:

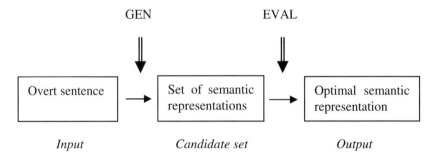

Figure 4 Interpretive optimization

In Chapter 4, these two directions of optimization will be combined into one bidirectional model. For the moment, however, it is sufficient to note that the same set of constraints with the same ranking (i.e. the same EVAL function) can be used to evaluate the candidate set in productive optimization and in interpretive optimization. Because the input and hence the candidate set differs in the two directions of optimization, applying the same set of constraints to the candidate set will have a different effect on production than on interpretation. Furthermore, only two levels of representation need to be assumed in productive and interpretive optimization. In each direction of optimization, an input level and an output level are sufficient. In the ideal case, the output level of the one type of optimization corresponds to the input level of the other type of optimization and vice versa. In principle, no intermediate levels of syntactic representation, comparable to LF in minimalist theory, are necessary.

Let us for simplicity assume that Kennedy's optimization at PF corresponds to productive optimization and Kennedy's optimization at LF corresponds to interpretive optimization. If the ranking of the constraints in EVAL would differ in productive and interpretive optimization, we would need to distinguish between a 'speaker grammar' and a 'hearer grammar'. As we already said, this is not a desirable result. Fortunately, if the same constraint hierarchy that is involved in optimizing over forms is also involved in optimizing over meanings, we get the same results as with Kennedy's two grammars. The function GEN maps an input representation to the set of all candidate outputs containing this input. Because productive optimization and interpretive optimization start with different inputs, they consider different candidate sets. Constraints such as DELETE and STAY are only relevant for the form of the sentence. To see this, recall that no intermediate levels of syntactic representation are assumed. As a result, there can be no covert syntactic movement. Hence, STAY does not have any effect on the interpretation of the sentence. Because DELETE and STAY are only relevant for the form of the sentence, they are **vacuously satisfied** by all competitors when determining the optimal interpretation. Similarly, RECOVERABILITY is vacuously satisfied in interpretation. Because RECOVERABILITY, as it is formulated by Kennedy, is a condition on the application of deletion, this constraint is not relevant for interpretation either.

So neither DELETE, nor STAY, nor RECOVERABILITY is relevant for the interpretation of the sentence. The result is that the weaker constraint C-SCOPE becomes important in choosing among several candidate interpretations. This constraint is relevant for the form as well as for the interpretation of the sentence. With respect to the form of the sentence, it requires compared constituents to appear in a scope taking position, that is, in the specifier position of the *than*-clause. With respect to the interpretation of the sentence, it requires compared constituents to be interpreted as taking clausal scope. If a compared constituent in the *than*-clause is taken to leave behind a variable which it binds, the *than*-clause can then be interpreted as a definite description, which is the interpretation Kennedy assumes for these constructions. For example, under Kennedy's semantic analysis the *than*-clause in (16) is represented as $max\{n \mid \exists X[tattoos(X) \wedge have(Dennis\_Rodman, X) \wedge \text{MANY}(X) \geq n\}$, where *max* is a maximality operator, X is a variable over pluralities, and MANY is a function from plural objects to amounts. This representation can be informally paraphrased as *the number of tattoos Dennis Rodman has*. Crucially, no such definite description results if the compared constituent does not take clausal scope because, in that case, the verb combines with the direct object directly, yielding *have(Dennis_Rodman, tattoos)*.

Both in CD constructions and in CSD constructions, therefore, the optimal semantic representation is one in which the compared constituent is interpreted as having clausal scope. So we do not need two separate grammars to account for the similarity in interpretation between CD constructions and CSD constructions. Rather, a similar result is obtained in a framework which assumes productive optimization and interpretive optimization to be subject to the same set of constraints with the same ranking. Bidirectional OT is such a framework.

A second problem with Kennedy's analysis of comparative formation concerns the status of the constraint RECOVERABILITY. In Kennedy's analysis, this constraint is phrased as a condition on production. Its effect is that deletion is only allowed if it is recoverable. However, given its dependence on the notion of semantic identity, RECOVERABILITY is not purely a condition on sentence form. The underlying idea behind this constraint is that deletion of a constituent is only possible if it is semantically identical to some other constituent. In a system in which production and interpretation proceed independently, constraints such as RECOVERABILITY are only possible if semantic identity is marked syntactically. In fact, this is Kennedy's approach to obligatory deletion as well as optional ellipsis. As we saw in the previous section, the compared constituent in the *than*-clause of a CD construction is syntactically marked as being identical to the head of the comparative by virtue of its syntactic position, namely SpecCP. As a result, the compared constituent must undergo obligatory deletion. With respect to optional ellipsis, Kennedy assumes that the semantic relation of identity is reflected in syntax by the distribution of E-features (cf. Merchant, 2001). E-features are syntactic features that may optionally be assigned to certain heads. In Merchant's analysis, an E-feature has different interpretations at the two interface levels. At LF, it is interpreted as a specification that the complement of the marked head stands in a semantic identity relation to some other constituent in the discourse. At PF, this feature is interpreted as an instruction to delete. In Kennedy's analysis, this latter function is taken over by the violable constraint DELETE.

Because of the introduction of E-features, Kennedy is able to formulate the constraint RECOVERABILITY in terms of grammatical identity rather than semantic identity. However, marking semantic properties by syntactic means does not seem to provide us with promising new insights. In addition, it obscures the distinction between form and meaning.

Interestingly, Kuhn (2003) shows that recoverability effects automatically follow in a bidirectional optimization model, in which the meaning of the reduced form is also taken into account. In a bidirectional system that aims at avoiding unnecessary structure (i.e., in which economy constraints such as STAY and DELETE play a role) we do not only have to check whether the reduced string is the optimal way of expressing the underlying meaning. We also have to check whether the underlying meaning is the optimal meaning for the reduced string. If the reduced string indeed is the optimal way of expressing the underlying meaning, and if the reduced string does not have another, more harmonic meaning, then deletion and anaphora are recoverable (see also Buchwald et al., 2002, and Vogel, 2004). On the other hand, if the reduced string yields a different meaning, the pair of form and meaning is not an optimal form-meaning pair. In this case, the nonreduced form will be a better way of expressing the underlying meaning. Another way to formulate this effect is to say that, in the latter case, deletion is not recoverable.

Now consider CD construction (14) and CSD construction (17), repeated below as (20) and (21). Clearly, if we delete the compared element in a CSD construction, for example *tattoos* in sentence (21), the optimal meaning is not its underlying meaning. Rather, the optimal meaning of the reduced sentence, which is now identical to CD construction (20), is one in which the deleted compared element is interpreted as identical to the head of the comparative construction, *scoring titles*.

(20) Michael Jordan has more scoring titles than Dennis Rodman has.

(21) Michael Jordan has more scoring titles than Dennis Rodman has tattoos.

Although sentence (20) has a more economical form than (21), it does not have the meaning of (21) as its optimal interpretation. The form in which no comparative deletion has applied, sentence (21), preserves the underlying meaning and hence is the optimal way to express this meaning. As a consequence, comparative deletion will not be possible in CSD constructions. So if we adopt a bidirectional optimization approach, we do not need a separate constraint on the recoverability of deleted constituents. The effect of bidirectional optimization is that, given a certain input meaning, constituents can only be deleted if interpretive optimization of the reduced form gives us the same meaning back again. Recoverability effects thus automatically follow from the interaction between productive optimization and interpretive optimization.

3

Compositionality

3.1 Introduction

In the previous chapter it was pointed out that the widely spread phenomenon of optionality in natural language is in fact problematic to explain within an OT framework. This chapter starts out with the investigation of a well-known instantiation of optionality in Dutch, *viz* the occurrence of a definite direct object either to the right or to the left of a sentential adverb, generally captured under the comprehensive term **scrambling**. We will show that in general there are two positions available for definite direct objects in Dutch. We will argue that an adequate analysis of the phenomenon of truly optional scrambling not only requires us to account for the existence of two forms, but also to account for the fact that these forms do not necessarily correspond to two available meanings in a one to one mapping. Rather, in order to account for the Dutch data, we have to properly distinguish two directions of optimization, one from meaning to form (productive optimization), the other one from form to meaning (interpretive optimization).

Subsequently, we will explore in detail the framework of OT semantics, and take up the issue of compositionality. In order to obtain the intended interpretation for quantified, but incomplete or anaphoric expressions, a compositional interpretation based on syntactic structure alone is often not possible. Information from the lexicon and from the context must be taken into account, and sometimes even overrules information from the syntactic structure. Given the notion of parallel evaluation of constraints of a different nature, we arrive at a truly cross-modular perspective on OT semantics. Not surprisingly, then, the different types of constraints may be in conflict with each other: a syntactically optimal interpretation may be pragmatically unlikely and the other way around. When syntax wins, we may say that compositionality is satisfied, while when pragmatics wins, we speak of a violation of compositionality. Towards the end of the chapter, we will argue that compositionality matters must be related to bidirectional optimization. Bidirectional OT guarantees a general procedure of optimization from form to meaning within a certain context and from meaning to form within a certain context such that the speaker's optimal expression of a meaning and the hearer's optimal interpretation of a form depend on each other in a well-defined way.

Finally, we will come back to the phenomenon of scrambling in Dutch, and illustrate the general idea of bidirectional OT with the marking and interpretation of indefinite and pronominal noun phrases.

3.2 Scrambling of Definites: Productive and Interpretive Optimization

In this section we will investigate the phenomenon of optional scrambling of definite noun phrases in Dutch. We argue that for the analysis we need to take into account the speaker perspective (productive optimization) as well as the hearer perspective (interpretive optimization).

3.2.1 Optional Scrambling of Definites in Dutch

In the literature on scrambling in Dutch, the object position to the right of a sentential adverb is called the unscrambled position, the one to the left of the adverb the scrambled position. Hence, (1b) is called the scrambled counterpart of the unscrambled word order in (1a).[1] In this section we will focus on optional scrambling of definite noun phrases, such as in (1) below, and we will argue that this type of word order variation in connection with the preferred interpretations in certain contexts can be adequately modeled using the notion of optimization not only in syntax but also in semantics. In the sentences under (1) scrambling is optional. That is, the sentences (1a) and (1b) are equally well-formed and share one and the same meaning:

(1) a. *Maar we moeten eerst de vogels waarschuwen.*[2]

---

[1] Special thanks go to Kyle Wohlmut for the translation of the Dutch text fragments.

[2] Examples in italics are taken from a Dutch children's book, *Otje*, by Annie M.G. Schmidt, Amsterdam: Querido, 1999.

but we must first the birds warn

b. Maar we moeten de vogels eerst waarschuwen.
   but we must the birds first warn

'But first we have to warn the birds.'

The paradigm in (1) is an illustration of the fact that definite object noun phrases in Dutch scramble freely. In this respect, definites behave differently from both indefinites and pronouns. Whereas scrambling of an indefinite is highly restricted, scrambling of a pronoun is almost obligatory. Two examples illustrate these claims concerning indefinites and pronouns. On the one hand, in (2a) the indefinite *een brief* ('a letter') must remain in situ since scrambling gives rise to an ill-formed sentence (2b). On the other hand, leaving a pronoun in situ results in an ill-formed sentence (3a). The pronoun *het* ('it') has to scramble, witness (3b).

(2) *Af en toe bleef hij stilstaan en keek peinzend naar de tafel.*

    a. *Ik heb hier vannacht toch een brief zitten schrijven, dacht hij.*
       I have here last night AFF a letter sit write thought he
    b. ?*Ik heb een brief hier vannacht toch zitten schrijven, dacht hij.
       I have a letter here last night AFF sit write thought he

Een brief aan Riekje. En nou ligt die brief er niet meer. Of heb ik soms gedroomd dat ik die brief schreef?

'Now and again he stopped and looked pensively at the table. I was sitting here writing a letter last night, he thought. A letter to Riekje. And now the letter isn't there anymore. Or perhaps I dreamed that I wrote the letter?'

(3) *De schrijver Marius Mengel zat moedeloos op zijn hotelkamer. Hij zocht niet langer naar zijn verloren papieren. 'Dat hoofdstuk is weg,' zei hij somber.*

    a. ?*'Ik moet helemaal overnieuw het schrijven.'
       I must all over-again it write
    b. *'Ik moet het helemaal overnieuw schrijven.'*
       I must it all over-again write

'The writer Marius Mengel sat dejectedly in his hotel room. He no longer looked for his lost papers. "That chapter is gone," he said somberly. "I have to write it all over again." '

Examination of the examples (1)-(3) reveals that definites behave as if they are in the middle of a **scrambling scale**, where indefinites are at one end and pronouns at the other. In fact, this observation is reminiscent of Givón's (1983) scale of the structural encoding of topicality, starting with the highest degree of topicality and going down the scale:

(4) Zero anaphora > weak pronouns > strong pronouns > right-detachment > neutral order + definite NPs > left-detachment > clefts > indefinite NPs

The correspondence with scrambling is striking. Therefore, it is tempting to try to account for the scrambling data in (1)-(3) in terms of topicality, too. That is, we know that pronouns are more topical than definites while definites in turn are more topical than indefinites. We might attempt to analyze scrambling phenomena in terms of discourse status (topic, focus) or discourse referentiality (anaphor, non-anaphor) instead of in terms of syntactic form (definite, indefinite).

One possible condition that springs to mind is a condition dubbed 'NEW' by Choi (1996). Choi's condition NEW requires that a [-new] (i.e. old) element precedes a [+new] (i.e. new) element. Choi investigates scrambling among arguments in German (i.e. the precedence relations among subjects, direct objects, and indirect objects), while we are concerned with the scrambling between direct objects and adverbs. Therefore, in de Hoop (2000; 2003) Choi's condition is reformulated as follows:

(5) NEW: Anaphors scramble.[3]

Let us now return to our examination of definite NPs. As we pointed out above, definites are in the middle of a scale: they are interpreted as anaphors more often than indefinites but less often than pronouns. Definite NPs can

---

[3] Note that we use the term *anaphor* rather than *topic*. Both anaphors and topics are often defined in terms of deaccentuation. Yet, not all anaphors are sentence or discourse topics. It is well-known that objects are less often topics than subjects. Still, anaphoric object NPs in Dutch tend to scramble, even when they are not topics, therefore the notion *anaphor* better captures the Dutch scrambling data than the notion *topic*.

occur in both scrambled and unscrambled positions in Dutch, usually without any effect on the grammaticality or well-formedness of the sentence. The condition NEW in (5) predicts that this optionality is more apparent than real and that the context determines whether a definite should be in scrambled or unscrambled position, in accordance with the claims made by Choi (1996) and Neeleman and Reinhart (1998). Although indeed many text examples appear to confirm the condition NEW, it should be noted that in the children's book *Otje* de Hoop (2003) also found examples that falsify NEW. One example of an anaphoric definite in unscrambled position is presented in (6a).

(6) *'En wordt de poes uit de brand gered?' vroeg Otje. 'Dat weet ik nog niet,' zei de schrijver. (...) 'Ik mag alles verzinnen wat ik wil.*

    a. *Ik wou eigenlijk de kat laten omkomen bij de brand.'*
        I would actually the cat let die in the fire
    b. Ik wou de kat eigenlijk laten omkomen bij de brand.'
        I would the cat actually let die in the fire

    ' "And is the cat saved from the fire?" asked Otje. "I don't know that yet," said the writer. (...) "I can make up anything I want. I would actually let the cat die in the fire." '

Additionally, an example of a non-anaphoric definite in scrambled position is provided in (7b), taken from an out of the blue context:

(7) a. Denk erom dat je nooit de muizen los laat lopen,' zeiden de tantes telkens weer.
        think about-it that you never the mice freely let run said the aunts again and again
    b. *'Denk erom dat je de muizen nooit los laat lopen,' zeiden de tantes telkens weer.*
        think about-it that you the mice never freely let run said the aunts again and again

    ' "Make sure that you never let the mice run freely," said the aunts again and again.'

In other words, scrambling of definites appears to be truly optional in Dutch. Moreover, Dutch native speakers agree that replacement of one word order variant by the other is allowed in all the above cases where definite noun phrases are involved. But if anaphoric definites as well as non-anaphoric definites freely alternate between the scrambled and the unscrambled position in Dutch, then NEW cannot adequately describe scrambling in Dutch. In de Hoop (2003) an alternative analysis is given for the inconsistent scrambling behavior of definites in Dutch.

3.2.2 An OT Syntactic Analysis of Scrambling Definites

In the literature it is usually assumed that the unscrambled word order is the unmarked or canonical word order in Dutch. So, if a noun phrase does not scramble, it satisfies the constraint STAY that was already introduced in Chapter 2 (cf. Choi, 1996; cf. Grimshaw, 1997). Here we use a slightly different formulation to focus on the phenomenon of scrambling.

(8) STAY: No scrambling.

Obviously, an anaphoric object will give rise to a conflict between the conditions NEW and STAY. Dependent on which one is stronger in a certain language, anaphors will either scramble (NEW » STAY) or stay in situ (STAY » NEW). A third possibility is that the constraints are equally strong, in which case we expect optional scrambling. This is how Choi (1996) accounts for the optionality of scrambling of certain noun phrases. However, NEW and STAY cannot account for the fact that sometimes non-anaphoric NPs scramble as well. If NEW and STAY were the only active constraints with respect to scrambling in Dutch, non-anaphoric NPs would never scramble. This is not the case, however, as we have seen. Hence, a third constraint has to be involved. STAY is a constraint that disfavors scrambled structures in general. However, we noticed that frequency and well-formedness of scrambling is partly a matter of the syntactic shape or semantic type of the NP irrespective of its discourse status (being an anaphor or not). That is, pronouns almost obligatorily scramble, whereas indefinites prefer to stay in situ. Finally, definites freely scramble, but they do scramble more often than not. Therefore, we may use the following constraint that obviously conflicts with STAY (de Hoop, 2000; 2003):

(9) SCRAMBLING 1 (SC1): Definite NPs scramble.

In an OT-syntactic analysis the input is a semantic representation, while the candidate outputs are a set of syntactic structures. The optimal syntactic structure (the winner) is the structure that best satisfies the different constraints. In OT syntax only optimal structures are grammatical. This means that when the input contains an anaphoric definite in Dutch, both the scrambled and the unscrambled output structure have to be optimal, since they are both well-formed. This can be represented in an OT syntax tableau:

TABLEAU 1
From anaphoric definite to optimal scrambling

Anaphoric definite	Sc1	New	Stay
☞ + scrambling			*
☞ - scrambling	*	*	

The input in Tableau 1 gives rise to two optimal output structures, a scrambled and an unscrambled structure. To account for this pattern, we have to assume that the three constraints are not ranked with respect to each other in Dutch, or, they are equally strong. In OT it is not important how many constraints an output violates, only the strengths of the violated constraints matter.

Although we are now able to explain why there are two optimal output structures for an input containing an anaphoric definite, this is not yet totally satisfactory. In fact, it would be more satisfactory if we could also account for the fact that we observe a strong tendency to satisfy NEW. That is, anaphoric definites very often scramble after all: they certainly scramble more often than not. Clearly, the analysis represented in Tableau 1 above does not explain this tendency. It only accounts for the observation that both output structures are well-formed in the case of an anaphoric definite.

One possibility to deal with that tendency is explored in de Hoop (2000, 2003) who adopts the partial ranking model of Anttila and Cho (1998), by which it is predicted that 2/3 of the anaphoric definites scramble. De Hoop's analysis accounts for the fact that even if scrambling is in principle free for anaphoric definites, we do scramble them more often than we leave them in situ.

Let us now consider the case of non-anaphoric definites. In general, it seems easier to scramble non-anaphoric definites than to leave anaphoric ones in situ. This is explained by the fact that NEW, a condition that plays an important part in the scrambling behavior of anaphoric definites, is not activated in the case of non-anaphoric definites. Hence, it is vacuously satisfied when the input contains a non-anaphoric definite. This leaves only the conflicting constraints STAY and Sc1 to affect the scrambling behavior of non-anaphoric definites, as illustrated in the following tableau:

TABLEAU 2
From non-anaphoric definite to optional scrambling

Non-anaphoric definite	Sc1	NEW	STAY
☞ + scrambling			*
☞ - scrambling	*		

Both output candidates are winners, since the constraints Sc1 and STAY are not ranked with respect to each other. Moreover, the model of Anttila and Cho (1998) predicts scrambling of a non-anaphoric definite in 50% of the cases.

3.2.3 An OT Semantic Analysis of Scrambling Definites

If indeed definite NPs are free to scramble or not, only partly dependent on their anaphoricity, then how come hearers/readers in Dutch never interpret these definites wrongly? Hearers are able to correctly assign anaphoric interpretations to definites in both scrambled and unscrambled position. Similarly, non-anaphoric definites are interpreted correctly, again irrespective of scrambling (see also de Hoop, 2000). We assume that this can easily be explained by distinguishing productive from interpretive optimization (Hendriks & de Hoop, 2001).

Word order conditions such as Sc1 and STAY are not relevant conditions in OT semantics, since they are violated or satisfied already at input level, hence they cannot affect the candidate outputs (scrambled or non-scrambled forms) for a certain input. NEW is important, because in interpretive optimization it is violated whenever an unscrambled definite gets an anaphoric interpretation. However, there is another constraint involved here which obviously outranks NEW. This stronger constraint favors anaphoric interpretations and was already introduced in Chapter 1, called DOAP by Williams (1997). It is repeated below for convenience:

(10) DOAP: Don't Overlook Anaphoric Possibilities. Opportunities to anaphorize text must be seized.

DOAP is a general pragmatic constraint that is satisfied whenever a noun phrase is interpreted anaphorically. In other words, when there is a potentially anaphoric noun phrase and a potential linguistic antecedent, then DOAP requires a referential link between the antecedent and the anaphor. As we have shown in Chapter 1, DOAP is violable. In Section 3.3.5 we provide an temporal variant of DOAP that can also be violated in favor of a stronger constraint. DOAP, being an interpretive constraint, applies to noun phrases independently of their syntactic position (scrambled or unscrambled). Thus, we obtain the anaphoric interpretation as the optimal (i.e. only) interpretation for the definite in (11), whether it has been scrambled or not.

> (11) a. Hij (...) greep de agent bij z'n das en zou stellig de arme man ge-
> wurgd hebben als niet...
> he (...) grabbed the officer by his tie and would certainly the poor
> man strangled have if not
>
> b. Hij (...) greep de agent bij z'n das en zou de arme man stellig ge-
> wurgd hebben als niet...
> he (...) grabbed the officer by his tie and would the poor man cer-
> tainly strangled have if not
>
> 'He (...) grabbed the officer by his tie and would have certainly
> strangled the poor man, if not for...'

In (11) it is impossible to interpret *de arme man* ('the poor man') as referring to an individual other than the individual referred to by the potential antecedent *de agent* ('the officer'). This optimal interpretation holds for the scrambled object in (11b) as well as the unscrambled one in (11a), which proves that DOAP must be stronger than NEW. The optimal anaphoric interpretation of (11a) violates NEW, but this is not a fatal violation: NEW must be violated in (11a) in order to satisfy DOAP. The other (non-anaphoric) interpretation would violate DOAP. Because there is a better candidate interpretation available, the interpretation that violates DOAP is not available for (11a) (hence, the officer and the poor man have to be one and the same guy). This is illustrated in Tableau 3.

TABLEAU 3
From optimal scrambling to anaphoric interpretation

Linguistic antecedent + scrambled definite	DOAP	NEW
☞ anaphoric interpretation		
non-anaphoric interpretation	*!	
Linguistic antecedent + unscrambled definite	DOAP	NEW
☞ anaphoric interpretation		*
non-anaphoric interpretation	*!	

3.2.4 Concluding Remarks

In this section we discussed an OT analysis for the truly optional scrambling of definite objects in Dutch, an analysis that was proposed by de Hoop (2000, 2003). The analysis does not predict random distribution of scrambling in the case of definite noun phrases, but it captures the general tendency of anaphoric definites to scramble. Moreover, by distinguishing between productive and interpretive optimization, it also explains why optional scrambling does not affect the interpretation of anaphoric definites.

One remaining problem for this analysis, however, seems to be that it crucially accounts for data concerning a certain class of noun phrases (definites) that allow for (nearly) free variation. It is not a trivial problem to extend the analysis in such a way that it can account for the highly restricted scrambling possibilities of indefinite noun phrases and pronouns. For example, if we would assume a word order constraint such as 'Pronouns do scramble' then we cannot account for the fact that this constraint is hardly ever violated, unless we assume that this constraint is stronger than STAY, but then we would predict obligatory scrambling of pronouns. However, we do find cases where pronouns stay in situ, but this always induces a 'special meaning effect'. The same but reverse holds for indefinites. A word order constraint that states that indefinite noun phrases do not scramble, could not explain the cases where a scrambled indefinite object and a special meaning go hand in hand. In Section 3.5 we will revisit the phenomenon of scrambling in Dutch, and argue that a proper analysis involves adopting a bidirectional perspective, along the lines of Blutner (2000). But before that, in Section 3.3 we will first take a closer look at the framework of OT semantics, that was already briefly introduced above.

3.3 Optimality Theoretic Semantics

Optimality Theory (OT) was developed in the 1990s by Alan Prince and Paul Smolensky as a general theory of language and grammar. Only recently OT was applied to semantic and pragmatic analysis for the first time and the last few years have shown a remarkable growth in the use of conflicting constraints to characterize natural language interpretation, as illustrated for example by the articles contained in a special issue of *Journal of Semantics* on OT semantics (Anttila & Fong, 2000; Blutner, 2000; Dekker & van Rooy, 2000; Geurts, 2000; ter Meulen, 2000; Zeevat, 2000). In OT semantic theory developed by Hendriks and de Hoop (Hendriks & de Hoop, 1997; 2001), each grammatical expression is associated with an, in principle, infinite number of interpretations. These candidate interpretations are tested against the ranked constraints in a parallel fashion. One of the advantages of such an approach is that constraints of various nature (syntactic, pragmatic, etc.) interact with each other in a truly cross-modular way. This view crucially differs from the classical compositional approach, where one interpretation is computed on the basis of the syntactic input, making use of context only when necessary. Whereas OT syntax optimizes syntactic structure with respect to a semantic input (the so-called speaker perspective), OT semantics optimizes interpretation with respect to a syntactic input (the hearer perspective). In Chapter 2 we concluded that bidirectional OT is required to account for recoverability effects. After our discussion of OT semantics in this chapter, we will integrate productive and interpretive optimization and argue again in favor of bidirectional OT, where the speaker and the hearer perspectives are taken simultaneously.

3.3.1 Compositionality and the Role of Context

The basic hypothesis advocated in Hendriks and de Hoop (2001) is that natural language interpretation can be characterized as an optimization problem. They claim that this novel view on interpretation accounts for the crucial role of contextual information while avoiding certain well-known problems associated with compositionality. The approach takes as a point of departure free generation of interpretations in combination with the parallel evaluation of violable constraints. The integration of pragmatic and syntactic/semantic information in a system of ranked constraints is proposed to correctly derive the optimal interpretations for inputs that contain nominal anaphors, determiner quantifiers, and elliptical comparatives.

Consider the following two sentences.

(12) Most people drink at night.

(13) Most people sleep at night.

The syntactic structures of the sentences in (12) and (13) are absolutely identical. Yet, in the absence of further context we might come up with two essentially different interpretations for the two sentences. On the one hand, sentence (12) is readily interpreted as a statement on when people usually drink. Hence, this reading could be paraphrased as 'Most people who drink, drink at night.' On the other hand, a natural interpretation of (13) involves a statement on what people usually do at night. 'At night, most people sleep.' Determiners such as *most* relate two sets of individuals. In the case of *most* the relation between the two sets A and B must be such that the number of elements in the intersection of the two sets (i.e. $|A \cap B|$) exceeds the number of elements in the difference of the two sets (i.e. $|A-B|$). The first set A is usually called the domain of quantification of the determiner. Say that *most* in (12) quantifies over the set of drinking people, while in (13) it quantifies over the set of people at night. Suppose a situation when half of the people drink (that is, they are drinkers) and 80% of these drinkers only drink at night. In that case (12) is true. Note that at the same time, (13) can be true as well, namely if the people who don't drink at night (the drinkers as well as the non-drinkers) sleep instead. In that particular situation with the two intended interpretations of (12) and (13), *Most people drink at night* and *Most people sleep at night* can be simultaneously true, although nobody drinks and sleeps at the same time.

In order to get the right truth conditions for the sentences (12) and (13) in the situation described above, we need to be able to restrict the domain of quantification of *most* in varying ways. The set of people must be intersected with the set of drinking individuals in (12) but with the set of individuals doing things at night in (13). The question is whether this can be done in a compositional way. Obviously, the syntactic structures of (12) and (13) are the same, so that syntax cannot be of help here. We might argue that focus interferes, in that the intended interpretation of (12) is obtained when *at night* is focused, while the interpretation we would like to derive for (13) depends on focusing *sleep*.

(14) Most people drink AT NIGHT.

(15) Most people SLEEP at night.

Accordingly, we obtain the interpretations the other way around if we switch the intonation patterns, as in (16) and (17).

(16) Most people DRINK at night.

(17) Most people sleep AT NIGHT.

(16) may be used as an answer to the question why there are so many empty beds in the middle of the night. The sentence in (17) could be uttered in a situation when you find somebody sleeping behind his desk during the day.

However, arguing that the focus or accent triggers the right interpretations in (12) and (13) is not very explanatory. Rather, focus seems to be in accordance with the intended interpretations, and not the other way around. That is, focus emerges as part of the interpretation or, we might say, it follows from the context in which the intended interpretation is obtained. As long as there is no independent mechanism that can predict accentuation of *at night* in (12) and *sleep* in (13), focus is not the trigger but instead is triggered by the preferred interpretations one obtains in (12) and (13). Hence, in the absence of further context, in the absence of a difference in syntactic configuration and in the absence of intonational clues, we must conclude that the different readings for (12) and (13) can only be the result of a difference between the lexical content of the sentences in combination with our world knowledge. As there is no structurally based, mechanical way in which the right interpretations can be derived, quantificational sentences like these are considered a problem for the semantic principle of compositionality, which states that the meaning of a complex expression is derived from the meanings of its parts in combination with the syntactic structure of the expression.

In fact, it can be argued that context always restricts the domain of quantification and hence, that in order to calculate the truth conditions of a quantificational expression, one always has to take into account the context.

(18) Most people drink.

(19) Most lazy people that smoke and have a cat drink.

(20) Most of them drink.

(21) Most drink.

(22) Most do.

The truth conditions of sentence (18) depend on what subset of people counts as the domain of quantification of *most*. Is it the set of all the people in the world, or is it a subset of people present at a certain party at a certain moment at which sentence (18) is uttered? In (19) lexical material is added that restricts the set of people over which *most* quantifies. But again, we may be dealing with the set of all the lazy people in the world that smoke and have a cat, or just a subset of them in a particular context. Obviously, (20) will have varying truth conditions depending on what the pronoun *them* refers to. If (21) is uttered out of the blue, the hearer totally depends on the context in order to determine the relevant set of individuals for the quantifier to live on, all under the assumption that the speaker obeys the Gricean maxim *Be relevant*. In (22), both sets of individuals related by *most* have to be determined independently of the lexical material of the sentence itself before the truth of the sentence can be calculated.

At this point, consider the sentence in (23).

(23) Most drink AT NIGHT.

In (23) there is no nominal phrase to provide the quantificational domain of *most*. If we want to derive the interpretation of (23) compositionally, we must assume the presence of an empty noun phrase. The content of this empty structure denotes the whole domain of individuals and gets intersected with a context set variable (Westerståhl, 1985). But in fact, then we need two context set variables. One would be equated with the generalized union over the set of alternatives for the syntactic argument that contains the focus (de Hoop & Solà, 1996), so that the quantificational domain would be the set of individuals who drink at certain times. The other one would be equated with some additional context set, for example, the set of linguists in Berlin. Hence, in the event we get as the domain of quantification the set of drinking linguists in Berlin. But how many contextual restrictions can or should we add before we may calculate the truth conditions of a quantificational sentence? The question arises when, how and to what extent people use different guiding principles to arrive at the proper interpretation of a quantified expression in a given context. As we have seen, different readings do in fact involve different truth conditions. Therefore, we may say that compositionality is complemented by information in the context in a way that is itself not compositional.

A similar problem for compositionality arises with comparative constructions. Comparatives are typically analyzed as quantifiers over degrees. In such an analysis, the comparative morpheme (*more*, *less*, *fewer*, *as* or the comparative suffix *–er*) defines a relation between two degrees: one introduced by the matrix clause and one introduced by the comparative clause, i.e. the complement of *than* or *as*. Although full comparative clauses are possible, elliptical comparative clauses are more common. Indeed, comparative deletion constructions as in (25) and phrasal comparatives as in (26) occur more frequently than full comparatives as in (24) (Rayner & Banks, 1990). This difference is reflected in the fact that young children (4-6 years old) find it much easier to comprehend comparative deletion, comparatives, and phrasal comparatives than full comparatives (Snyder, Wexler, & Das, 1995). According to Rayner and Banks (1990) the most frequently occurring comparatives are in fact discourse comparatives, that is, comparatives lacking a *than*-clause or *than*-prase altogether, as in (27) below. Note that it is possible to omit even more material from a comparative construction. For example, (28) and (29) can be used in response to the utterance *Jacky ate fewer bananas than Jill*, and (30) is a possible correction of this statement: 'No, more!'

(24) Jane ate more bananas than Jacky ate apples.

(25) Jane ate more bananas than Jacky ate.

(26) Jane ate more bananas than Jacky.

(27) Jane ate more bananas.

(28) Jane ate more.

(29) Jane more.

(30) More!

So, ellipsis can take several forms in comparative constructions. The question is how we can arrive at a principled account of the interpretation of elliptical comparative constructions. Approaches to ellipsis resolution generally aim at either (re)constructing a syntactically complete or a semantically complete representation of the elliptical construction. Problematic for a deletion as well as a reconstruction account of ellipsis are cases in which the antecedent is syntactically non-identical to the elided material, as in (31) (Pinkham, 1982), compared to (32), or in which there is no overt antecedent (as in (33)).

(31) Mary ran faster than the world record (*ran).

(32) Mary ran faster than the world champion (ran).

(33) [context: Jane is standing in front of Jacky, holding a full pot of coffee. Jacky is just finishing the coffee in her cup] Jane: 'Would you like some more?'

Clearly, if no antecedent is overtly present in the linguistic context, there is no way the lacking material can be recovered or reconstructed.

Under a direct interpretation approach, as is for instance characteristic of categorial grammar, compositional interpretation is driven by the lexical semantics of the elements present in the sentence. Therefore, certain lexical elements have to be assigned a new semantic type for every new type of ellipsis. In view of the variation in ellipsis possible in comparatives (see (24)-(30) for only a few of the possibilities), this could result in an explosion of semantic types for one lexical element. Furthermore, cases like (31) and (33) above, in which there is no overt antecedent present in the sentence, constitute a major problem for direct interpretation approaches. These approaches account for the interpretation of elliptical sentences by reusing meanings that have been introduced elsewhere in the sentence, either by copying these meanings as part of the proof derivation (Jäger, 1997) or through unification of the anaphoric term and the antecedent term (Kennedy, 1997; Morrill, 1994). When there is no antecedent present in the sentence, however, there is no meaning that can be reused. As most comparatives are in fact discourse comparatives, such a situation is not exceptional at all. Consider the sequence of comparatives in (34). They all lack a *than*-phrase, yet we have no trouble whatsoever in interpreting the sentence.

(34) Die lockere Stadt schloß sich enger und enger um ihn, sie saugte ihn in sich hinein. Der Lärm wuchs, höher schienen sich die Häuser zu wachsen, grauer wurden ihre Fassaden, eiliger liefen die Menschen.
[Hans Fallada, *Ein Mann will nach oben*]

At this point, we may conclude that in many cases syntactic or lexical information is not sufficient to arrive at the correct interpretation of elliptical comparative constructions. The question arises what other factors determine interpretation in this domain. As we saw in the beginning of this section, the interpretation of quantified sentences is strongly influenced by world knowledge as well as intonation. This can also be observed in comparatives. Sentence (35), for example, has the preferred interpretation that Slonimsky hit more than sixty home runs last year, according to McCawley (1998), who terms this the 'atemporal stereotype' interpretation.

(35) Last year, Slammer Slonimsky hit more home runs than Babe Ruth.

But this interpretation only prevails if one knows that Babe Ruth died years ago, which makes a comparison between the number of home runs that Slonimsky hit last year and the number of home runs that Babe Ruth hit last year (namely zero) rather meaningless. Note that the preferred interpretation here involves a violation of the constraint on identity of the elliptical material and the antecedent material again (as was the case in (31) as well). In this case, the anaphoric clause must be interpreted outside the scope of the temporal adverb *last year*.

We claim that the information provided by the semantic relation itself is crucial to interpretation. This holds equally for a semantic relation expressed by a determiner such as *most* as for a semantic relation expressed by a comparative morpheme. In general, there seems to be no straightforward way to construe a compositional interpretation procedure for (elliptical) quantified constructions (i.e. for simple quantified sentences as well as for comparatives). Context, intonation, and syntax all interact in the determination of the argument structure of a semantic relation.

3.3.2   Compositionality: A Violable Constraint as well?

At this point, the aim is to develop an analysis of the possible interpretations of elliptical or anaphorical quantificational expressions. We will discuss several general constraints that govern interpretation. The constraints we discuss are not new; they have been linguistically motivated in the literature. What is new is of course our conception of these constraints as soft. We will show that these constraints must indeed be soft, since they can be overruled. The basic hypothesis of OT semantics is that when people interpret expressions, they try to satisfy the constraints the best they can and they only violate constraints when this allows them to satisfy the stronger ones.

Above we argued that sincere problems for compositionality arise whenever the truth-conditions of a sentence are determined beyond the lexical parts and its syntactic structure. We have seen that the truth-conditional meaning depends on context and world knowledge as well. Dekker and van Rooy (2000) recognize the problem of compositionality as well:

> The above example shows that we cannot systematically determine the semantic content of a sentence in a *compositional* way based on its syntactic structure, without making reference to the attitudes of speakers and hearers, if we equate the semantic content of a sentence with its truth-conditions. (Dekker & van Rooy, 2000: 220)

They discuss the strategy that should be followed, given this problem with compositionality:

> So what should we do? Give up compositionality, or give up the assumption that what should be determined compositionally are the truth-conditions of a sentence? The former, radical, option would result almost surely in giving up the distinction between semantics and pragmatics (…). According to the latter option, compositional semantics still has a role to play. However, the semantic content of a sentence is not fully determined and does not give rise to clearcut truth-conditions; it is left *underspecified*. (Dekker & van Rooy, 2000: 220)

Dekker and van Rooy seem to overlook a third option, one that does maintain compositionality, yet considerably weakens the distinction between semantics and pragmatics. The third alternative could be formulated as follows: maintain compositionality, but not as an absolute principle, but as a violable albeit strong constraint. Compositionality, then, is nothing but an instantiation of a faithfulness constraint, a constraint that preserves the input (lexical material as well as syntactic structure) in the output (interpretation). This is clearly also the approach taken by Zeevat (2000), who discusses two constraints, *INVENT (prohibits adding material to the content or context of utterance) and FAITH-INT (that requires us to interpret all that the speaker has said). Satisfaction of these two constraints means interpreting all and only the material available in the utterance, and so, their combination 'restores important aspects of compositional semantics (not the full principle, but essential aspects)' (Zeevat, 2000).

It goes without saying that compositionality as a soft constraint or set of constraints opens up a new way to analyze apparent violations of compositionality: in those cases, stronger constraints than compositionality are active. Metaphors might be analyzed as a special case of this. In the remainder of this chapter, we will only discuss interpretations where at least part of compositionality is satisfied (the part of the constraint that is dubbed FAITH-INT by Zeevat (2000)). However, towards the end of this chapter, we return to the issue of compositionality and argue that compositionality as a leading methodological guide in semantic interpretation can be maintained in a broader sense, as a result from the application of the constraints in a bidirectional way. Because compositionality can thus be considered an epiphenomenon of interacting violable (faithfulness) constraints, including violable syntactic constraints, it is a gradual phenomenon and can show up with varying strength.

3.3.3 Interpretive Optimization of Nominal Anaphora

Recall the general pragmatic constraint DOAP introduced in Chapter 1 and Section 3.2.3 above, which captures the fact that in the unmarked case, (sets of) individuals that are already available in the discourse are chosen as the implicit arguments of semantic relations denoted by determiners and comparatives. Below, we repeat DOAP once again for convenience.

(36) DOAP: Don't Overlook Anaphoric Possibilities. Opportunities to anaphorize text must be seized.

Let us now return to the argument selection of determiners, as discussed in Section 3.3.1 above. If no other constraints apply, then we expect DOAP to hold for quantified expressions as well. Consider the following example (boldface is ours):

(37) The buildings are all two and three stories running half a block deep with brick and glass fronts. **Most** were built together, **a few** have nar-

row alleys between them. **Many** are still boarded up, **a couple** were burned out years ago.

(John Grisham, *The Rainmaker*)

DOAP will ensure that the incomplete noun phrases in (37) try to establish an anaphoric relation with a linguistic antecedent. Here, the incomplete noun phrases are anaphorically linked to the accessible discourse topic *the buildings*. As pointed out by de Hoop and de Swart (2004) there is yet another meaning effect here. The pairs of predicates in the second and third sentence are interpreted **contrastively**. The interpretation that emerges is that buildings are either built together or have narrow alleys between them, and they are either still boarded up, or burned out years ago. Where does this reading come from?

Contrast is defined by Mann and Thompson (1988) as a multi-nuclear rhetorical relation with no more than two nuclei such that the situations presented in these two nuclei are (a) comprehended as the same in many respects (b) comprehended as differing in a few respects and (c) compared with respect to one or more of these differences. According to Mann and Thompson, the effect of Contrast is that the reader recognizes the comparability and the difference(s) yielded by the comparison being made. We consider Contrast to be one (quite popular) way of fulfilling DOAP in the rhetorical domain (de Hoop & de Swart, 2000), see also Sections 3.3.5 and 3.3.6 below. That is, hearers prefer to interpret discourses as being coherent, i.e., to make anaphoric links wherever possible. One way of satisfying coherence in the discourse is to establish a relation of Contrast. This can be formulated as a constraint:

(38) CONTRAST: Establish a rhetorical relation of Contrast between two situations.

To see how a constraint like CONTRAST influences discourse interpretation, consider the interpretations obtained in (39) and (40) (the examples are also discussed in Hendriks and de Hoop, 2001):

(39) Most students attended the meeting. Some spoke.

(40) Most deliveries were on time. Some weren't.

In (39) the preferred domain of quantification for the second determiner, *some*, is the set of students that attended the meeting (that is, the intersection of the sets A and B related by the first determiner, *most*). In (40), however, the domain of quantification for the second determiner, *some*, is not the set of deliveries that were on time, but the whole set of deliveries (set A of the first determiner, *most*). On the one hand, it is clear why the other reading is ruled out in (40). If *some* would quantify over the set of deliveries that were on time, we would get a contradictory interpretation, *viz.* that some deliveries that were on time weren't on time. On the other hand, in (39) we get the intersection reading in the absence of contrastive predicates that would trigger a contrastive reading.

We can explain the difference between the preferred interpretations in (39) and (40) in terms of the interaction between two constraints, CONTRAST and FORWARD DIRECTIONALITY (de Hoop & de Swart, 2004; Hendriks & de Hoop, 2001). In (40) we establish a relation of Contrast between most deliveries that were on time and some that were not on time. However, in (39) such a relation of Contrast is not possible. There is no contrast between the situation that most students attended the meeting and the situation that some students spoke. Hence, CONTRAST is violated for both candidate interpretations of (39). This does not mean that the discourse is incoherent. Satisfaction of a weaker constraint, FORWARD DIRECTIONALITY, saves the coherence of the discourse as well (cf. Hendriks and de Hoop, 2001):

(41) FORWARD DIRECTIONALITY: The original topic range induced by the domain of quantification of a determiner is reduced to the topic range induced by the intersection of the two argument sets of that determiner.

FORWARD DIRECTIONALITY favors the interpretation obtained in (39). In (40) FORWARD DIRECTIONALITY is violated. If we assume that CONTRAST is ranked above FORWARD DIRECTIONALITY, we account for the right preferred interpretation in (40). Note furthermore that satisfaction of CONTRAST goes hand in hand with satisfaction of PARALLELISM, which was argued to be ranked below FORWARD DIRECTIONALITY by Hendriks and de Hoop (2001).

(42) PARALLELISM: As the antecedent of an anaphoric expression, choose a parallel element from the preceding clause.

Thus, as the reader may verify, the ranking in (43) accounts for the proper interpretations of the sentences in (37) and (39)-(40):

(43) CONTRAST » FORWARD DIRECTIONALITY » PARALLELISM

Note that the three constraints introduced above are all interpretive constraints. They guide the hearer or reader towards the optimal interpretation of an expression. The first constraint CONTRAST states that the hearer tries to establish the rhetorical relation Contrast in the case of two (potentially) contrastive situations. The second constraint FORWARD DIRECTIONALITY favors topic narrowing from a set to a particular subset. Finally, the constraint PARALLELISM tells the hearer to look for a structurally parallel antecedent to which the anaphor can be linked.

3.3.4 Interpretive Optimization of Comparatives

In the previous section, we suggested that PARALLELISM is a violable and in fact rather weak constraint. As is well-known from the literature, parallelism plays an important role in the interpretation of ellipsis and anaphora (Dalrymple, Shieber, & Pereira, 1991; Gawron, 1995; Hobbs & Kehler, 1997; Prüst, 1992; Sag & Hankamer, 1984). Interpretations that respect parallel relations between anaphors and possible antecedents are to be preferred, but only as long as they are not ruled out by other, stronger, constraints. In our view, PARALLELISM is a constraint on interpretation in general, and not a property of the mechanism for ellipsis resolution. Indeed, as psycholinguistic experiments reveal, parallelism effects cannot be the result of LF-copying since they also occur with *do it* anaphors (Murphy, 1985; Tanenhaus & Carlson, 1990). These authors found that syntactic parallelism affects the speed with which both implicit VP anaphors and overt *do it* anaphors are interpreted, an effect that cannot be explained by assuming a distinction between the way 'surface' and 'deep' anaphors are being processed (Sag & Hankamer, 1984), but which seems to be in accordance with the Optimality Theoretic semantics approach defended here. That is, PARALLELISM reduces the set of candidate interpretations of a sentence to one, namely the parallel interpretation, in cases where no stronger constraints are in conflict with PARALLELISM. Note that if PARALLELISM is a violable constraint, it cannot determine the contrasted elements in a comparison in all cases, which appears to be exactly the result that we need.

At this point it should be pointed out that PARALLELISM is not a single constraint but rather a family of constraints. Different types of parallelism have been proposed in the literature that all seem to play a role in the interpretation of elliptical and anaphoric sentences: structural parallelism between an anaphoric element and its antecedent, thematic parallelism between these elements, parallelism in the linear order of these elements, focal parallelism, structural parallelism between the remaining material in an anaphoric clause and corresponding material in the antecedent clause, and parallelism between the attachment site of an anaphoric clause and of its antecedent clause. On the other hand, it has been observed that no notion of parallelism seems to hold in all cases (van Leusen, 1994; Williams, 1997). This already suggests that PARALLELISM must in fact be a family of violable constraints. In the remainder of this section, we will show the effects of PARALLELISM on the interpretation of comparatives.

We will restrict ourselves to comparatives without a comparative clause. In these elliptical comparatives, a comparison is made between a degree associated with an element which is left implicit but can be expressed by a *than*-clause in a non-elliptical comparative. This implicit contrasted element can be anaphoric to a structurally parallel element in the preceding sentence, as in (44):

(44) A: Jane is taller than Jacky.
B: No, Jane is shorter.

The incomplete comparative in (44) is anaphoric to the structurally parallel phrase *Jacky* in the preceding sentence. However, as the sentence in (45) shows, this does not always give us the correct interpretation.

(45) Jane smokes more than Jacky, but Jacky drinks more.

The interpretation that would be in accordance with PARALLELISM is the one that can be paraphrased as '…but Jacky drinks more than Jacky.' Obviously, this is not the optimal interpretation of the incomplete second conjunct in (45). The optimal interpretation is that Jacky drinks more than Jane. Here, PARALLELISM is in conflict with the constraint that a semantic relation (in this case, comparison) is always between two different elements, unless marked otherwise (i.e. PRINCIPLE B, introduced in Chapter 1, Section 1.5). To avoid violations of PRINCIPLE B, PARALLELISM must be violated. The only other present argument in the preceding sentence, *Jane*, is interpreted as the antecedent of the contrasted element in the second sentence, in accordance with DOAP. This shows that PARALLELISM is overruled by PRINCIPLE B.

That PARALLELISM is a violable constraint is confirmed by a series of psycholinguistic experiments run by Smyth (1994). These experiments show that pronoun resolution is subject to (at least) two interacting constraints. The first constraint that plays a role in pronoun resolution is PARALLELISM. The second one is a constraint that captures the fact that a subject is preferred as the antecedent of a pronoun (it might be important to note that all the subjects in Smyth's examples were topics).

We witnessed above that the constraint interaction between PARALLELISM and PRINCIPLE B governs the interpretation for comparatives without a comparative clause. Consider one more set of examples:

(46) Jane gave more presents to Jill than to Jacky, and ...
    a. Jill gave more presents to Jacky.
    b. Jill gave more presents to Mary.
    c. Jacky gave more presents to Jane.
    d. Jacky gave more presents to Mary.

The context sentence 'Jane gave more presents to Jill than to Jacky' is followed by four possible elliptical continuations in (46a-d). What are the interpretations obtained for these continuations? We asked several groups of students to give us their favorite interpretations before showing them the tableau below and the results were remarkably in accordance with the prediction on the basis of the interaction of the two proposed constraints. The interpretations that arise in the contexts of (46a-d) are all in accordance with DOAP, which we may safely omit from the analysis therefore, and they correspond to the following implicit continuations:

(47) Jane gave more presents to Jill than to Jacky, and ...
    a. Jill gave more presents to Jacky (than to Jane)
    b. Jill gave more presents to Mary (than to Jacky)
    c. Jacky gave more presents to Jane (than to Jill)
    d. Jacky gave more presents to Mary (than to Jane and to Jill)

The interpretations given in (47) are the interpretations that are optimal when we take into account the constraint hierarchy PRINCIPLE B » PARALLELISM as is illustrated below.

TABLEAU 4

The optimal interpretation of comparative clauses

(46a)	PRINCIPLE B	PARALLELISM
☞ ... than to Jane		*
... than to Jacky	*!	
... than to Jill	*!	*
(46b)	PRINCIPLE B	PARALLELISM
... than to Jane		*!
☞ ... than to Jacky		
... than to Jill	*!	*
(46c)	PRINCIPLE B	PARALLELISM
... than to Jane	*!	*
... than to Jacky	*!	
☞ ... than to Jill		*
(46d)	PRINCIPLE B	PARALLELISM
☞ ... than to Jane		*
... than to Jacky	*!	
☞ ... than to Jill		*

Continuation of (46a), for example, is interpreted as meaning that Jill gave more presents to Jacky than to Jane. Here, the explicit contrasted element of the context sentence is not chosen as the implicit contrasted element of the elliptical comparative, since obeying PARALLELISM would result in a violation of PRINCIPLE B. Because interpreting *Jill* as the contrasted element would also result in a violation of PRINCIPLE B, the best choice for the contrasted element in (46a) is *Jane*. In (46b), obeying PARALLELISM does not result in a violation of PRINCIPLE B. Therefore, the interpretation that Jill gave more presents to Mary than to Jacky is the preferred interpretation for this sentence. PARALLELISM is obeyed because no stronger constraints have to be violated in order to do so. On the other hand, obeying PARALLELISM in (46c) leads to a violation of PRINCIPLE B, as in (46a). The only possibility for the interpretation of the implicit contrasted element in (46c) is *Jill*, since this choice does not result in a violation of PRINCIPLE B, whereas choosing *Jane* again does. Finally, in (46d) neither the choice of *Jane* nor the choice of *Jill* conflicts with either of the two constraints. In principle, then, this sentence is ambiguous between the two readings predicted by the tableau. It must be noted, however, that in the absence of further disambiguation clues, the reading that is obtained is a combination of the two, namely that Jacky gave more presents to Mary than to Jane and Jill.

3.3.5 Interpretive Optimization of Temporal Anaphora

In de Hoop and de Swart (2000), an analysis is provided of the possible interpretations of temporal adjunct clauses inside and outside the scope of adverbial quantifiers. They focus on the contribution of *when*-clauses, and argue that the constraints they impose upon temporal anaphora play a crucial role in quantificational structure as well. The argument builds on the hypothesis advocated in Hendriks and de Hoop (1997, 2001) that the constraints that interact in determining the interpretation of sentences must be soft in nature, i.e. violable and potentially conflicting. The same hypothesis can be applied to the interpretation of *when*-clauses, using the insights and analysis developed in de Swart (1999) on the anaphoric character of constructions involving time adverbials. Next, the quantificational structure of adverbs of quantification can be determined using the same type of constraints on anaphoric relations.

In Chapter 1 we presented a tableau for the optimal anaphoric interpretations of definite and pronominal noun phrases using the constraints DOAP and PRINCIPLE B. Partee (1973) observed that tenses are similar to pronouns in their preference for anaphoric interpretations. This suggests that constraints like PRINCIPLE B and DOAP have a counterpart in the temporal domain. It turns out that temporal versions of these constraints govern the interpretation of constructions involving preposed and postponed temporal adjunct clauses.

Temporal adjunct clauses introduced by *when, before, after,* etc. come with tense and aspect. In this section, we will restrict ourselves to the interpretation of *when*-clauses; see de Swart (1999) for an extension of the analysis to other temporal connectives. Heinämäki (1978) observes that the intervals or moments denoted by accomplishments and achievements are included in the intervals referred to by durative sentences (48), while two durative sentences overlap (49) and two accomplishments happen in succession (50):

(48) Everybody was away when Jane destroyed the documents.

(49) It was raining in San Francisco when we were there.

(50) When Robert wrecked the car, Jane fixed it.

Heinämäki's claim that two events related by *when* happen in succession (cf. (50)) has been challenged. Partee (1984) argues that any temporal relation which can be established between two independent clauses can be established between the subordinate and the main clause related by the temporal connective *when*. However, the situation is more complicated than that. It is well known that the interpretation of temporal adjuncts is sensitive to clause order. De Swart (1999) observes that neither preposed nor postponed *when*-clauses express a succession of events in which the event described by the subordinate clause follows the main clause event, even if this is strongly suggested by world knowledge. However, 'follows' is to be interpreted not in the strictly temporal sense, but in a rhetorical or discourse sense. That is, *when*-clauses are never interpreted as the anaphor (the dependent element) in a rhetorical relation. Compare:

(51) When the president asked who would support her, Robert raised his hand.

(52) Robert raised his hand when the president asked who would support her.

(53) When Robert raised his hand, the president asked who would support her.

(54) The president asked who would support her when Robert raised his hand.

(55) The president asked who would support her. Robert raised his hand.

The preposed *when*-clause in (51) allows for only one reading: the main clause event is located shortly after the event described by the adjunct clause. There is a strong causal connection between the two events: Robert's raising of his hand is naturally interpreted as a response to the president's request for support. The causal connection is indicative of a rhetorical structure (Lascarides & Asher, 1993). (53) is similar. World knowledge does not as easily support a causal connection here, but it is not impossible to imagine a scenario in which Robert's raising of his hand is a sign for the president that it is time to ask for support. Again, this interpretation can be taken to reflect a rhetorical relation between the two clauses. Postposition of the temporal clauses as in (52) and (54) leads to ambiguities. Under one reading of (52), the sentence is interpreted in the same way as (51). But there is an alternative interpretation available in which Robert raises his hand just at the moment at which the president asks who would support her. Under this reading there is no causal relation between the two actions; there is just a relation of temporal overlap. Similarly, (54) shares one reading with (53), but it has another interpretation in which we do not establish a causal connection or an enablement relation, but just posit a relation of temporal overlap. The puzzle is the lack of a reading for (54) along the lines of (51) or the sequence of independent clauses in (55). If two events related by *when* could describe the two events independently of subordination, then we would predict that we could locate Robert's raising of his hand after the president's request for support. After all, such a causal connection is strongly supported by world knowledge. However, such an interpretation of (54) is impossible. In this section, we will present an OT semantic analysis of the paradigm in (51)-(55) (de Hoop & de Swart, 2000).

An important difference between main clauses and temporal adjunct clauses resides in their anaphoric behavior. Main clauses are anaphoric just like independent clauses. This means that their temporal anchoring is determined by the relation with the preceding discourse. Following Lascarides and Asher's (1993) claim that temporal relations are derived from the rhetorical structure of the discourse, de Swart (1999) argues that main and independent clauses seek to establish a rhetorical relation with an earlier sentence in the discourse. A main or independent clause β thus tries to establish a rhetorical relation R with a clause α which is already part of the discourse representation structure built up so far. Both the nominal and the temporal domain thus have a preference for anaphoric interpretations. Accordingly, we propose a temporal version of DOAP, which we formulate as follows (note that we already introduced the constraint CONTRAST above, satisfaction of which would automatically involve satisfaction of the more generally formulated DOAP-R below.

(56) DOAP-R: Don't Overlook Anaphoric Possibilities. Opportunities to establish a rhetorical relation must be seized.

DOAP-R resembles the condition dubbed *Maximize discourse coherence* (Asher & Lascarides, 1998). The rhetorical version of DOAP is clearly satisfied in the discourse (55): the second clause takes the first one as its antecedent in a rhetorical relation. A mixture of linguistic information (aspect) and non-linguistic information (world knowledge about causal connections) decides which rhetorical relation is most appropriate in a given context. Temporal structure may then be inferred from rhetorical structure. In the case of (55), the causal connection leads to temporal succession. DOAP-R is also satisfied in (51) and (53): the *when*-clause provides the antecedent α for the main clause β, and we can establish a rhetorical relation R between α and β. The interpretations of (52) and (54) which they share with (51) and (53) respectively satisfy DOAP-R for the same reason. But what about the other reading of (52) and (54), in which there is no causal connection, but just a relation of temporal overlap? These cases show a conflict between DOAP-R and the non-anaphorical character of *when*-clauses, already mentioned above. That is, time adverbials never fulfill the role of β in a rhetorical relation R(α,β). De Hoop and de Swart call this constraint TA, and view it as a construction-specific restriction on anaphoric interpretations, in that sense comparable to PRINCIPLE B discussed in Chapter 1 and in Section 3.3.4 above.

(57) TA: Temporal adjuncts do not function as β in a rhetorical relation R(α,β).

In contexts in which the adjunct is not interpreted as the antecedent α, we cannot create a rhetorical structure. As argued by de Swart (1999), preposed temporal clauses always provide the rhetorical antecedent of the anaphoric main clause. A postponed *when*-clause either provides the rhetorical antecedent of the main clause, or it establishes a relation of temporal overlap in the absence of a rhetorical relation. Thus the constraints formulated in (56) and (57), which take care of the anaphoric possibilities of main and adjunct clauses, need to be combined with the difference in word order between preposed and postponed temporal adjunct clauses. De Hoop and de Swart introduce a correspondence constraint that reflects the general observation that antecedents precede anaphors in discourse.

(58) αβ: The linear order of two clauses corresponds to the order antecedent-anaphor in a rhetorical structure, i.e., αβ : R(α,β).

If we combine these constraints in a tableau, we can see that the optimal interpretation for the input sequence of a preposed *when*-clause is the result of the satisfaction of all three constraints. Consider Tableau 5, which we can take to represent the optimization process of examples like (51) and (53) above:

TABLEAU 5

The interpretation of a sentence containing a preposed *when*-clause

When-clause (e_1); main clause (e_2)	TA	DOAP-R	$\alpha\beta$
☞ $R(e_1,e_2)$			
$R(e_2,e_1)$	*!		*
¬R		*!	

What we see in Tableau 5 is that there is one interpretation which satisfies all three constraints. In this optimal interpretation, we establish a rhetorical relation (satisfaction of DOAP-R), without making the *when*-clause the rhetorical anaphor (satisfaction of TA), and the antecedent-anaphor order is reflected in the clause order (satisfaction of $\alpha\beta$). As a result, the optimal interpretation makes the *when*-clause the rhetorical antecedent for the main clause. Thus, in (51) for example, the president's request triggers Robert's raising of his hand as a natural response. An interpretation in which Robert raising his hand triggers the president's request is the optimal interpretation for (53), then. Other interpretations than the ones just sketched are not felicitous for these sentences, because they violate one or more of the constraints. This suggests that the combination of the three constraints yields a set of constraints that appropriately constrains the interpretation of preposed *when*-clause constructions. Note however that preposed *when*-clauses do not give us any clue as to the ranking of the three constraints. Obviously, cases in which the optimal candidate does not violate any constraints at all do not allow us to determine the ranking within a set of constraints. Quite generally, we need to look at cases in which there is a conflict between constraints in order to decide the ranking. Postponed *when*-clauses provide such a case. Consider Tableau 6 for the interpretation of examples like (52) and (54).

TABLEAU 6

The interpretation of a sentence containing a postponed *when*-clause

Main clause (e_2); *when*-clause (e_1)	TA	DOAP-R	$\alpha\beta$
☞ $R(e_1,e_2)$			*
$R(e_2,e_1)$	*!		
☞ ¬R		*	

Sentences containing postponed *when*-clauses generally allow two interpretations. One is the same interpretation as the construction with the preposed *when*-clause. But unlike in Tableau 5 with the preposed *when*-clause as input, this interpretation violates αβ. That is, the linear order of the main clause and the *when*-clause does not correspond to the order antecedent-anaphor in the rhetorical relation. The constraint αβ is satisfied by the second candidate, but this candidate violates TA, which is obviously a more serious violation as the concomitant interpretation does not occur. In the other possible interpretation, there is no rhetorical relation. What remains, then, is a relation of temporal overlap between the two events. This temporal relation is present, although it is not visible in the notation of the interpretation in the tableau, which only gives the relevant details for the purpose of the analysis (that is, concerning the possible existence of a rhetorical relation between the events described by the two clauses of the input). In an Optimality Theoretic approach, the fact that there are two interpretations available suggests that there are two optimal candidates. Such a situation typically arises when each output violates some condition, but the two conditions are ranked equally high. This is indeed the situation we find in Tableau 6. We have three constraints and we observe that a violation of TA never leads to an optimal interpretation. We can thus rank this constraint higher than DOAP-R. The two other interpretations each violate one constraint. If we give the sentence the same interpretation as its counterpart with a preposed *when*-clause, we satisfy DOAP-R but we violate αβ. If we do not establish a rhetorical relation but interpret *when* as temporal overlap, we satisfy αβ but we violate DOAP-R. If we rank these constraints equally high, but rank TA higher, we end up with the two desired interpretations as the optimal candidates.

In sum, we see that DOAP-R is a general constraint, which works in the temporal domain pretty much like in the domain of individuals (compare the discussion of the role of DOAP in nominal anaphora interpretation in Chapter 1 above). αβ is interesting in that it mixes syntactic (word order) and discourse semantic information in one constraint. Neither of these two constraints is specific to the *when*-construction. However, not all temporal expressions have the same anaphoric possibilities. This leads to the formulation of a construction-specific constraint TA. We find that DOAP-R and αβ can be overruled by TA. Hence, TA is ranked higher than DOAP-R and αβ. We think that the resulting picture provides an illustration of the power of OT semantics.

3.3.6　Adverbial Quantification

In the previous section, we accounted for the effects of preposed and post-poned *when*-clauses on the interpretation of the discourse. We will extend this analysis to account for the interpretation of these clauses within the quantificational structure of quantifying adverbs. Consider the following two sentences, borrowed from Rooth (1985):

(59) Martin usually shaves when he is in the bathroom.

(60) When he is in the bathroom, Martin usually shaves.

The generalization is as follows: preposed *when*-clauses always restrict the domain of quantification of the quantifying adverb, in this case *usually*. Postponed *when*-clauses are ambiguous. If focus is on the main clause (read: 'Martin usually SHAVES when he is in the bathroom'), the *when*-clause restricts the domain of quantification. If focus is on the *when*-clause (read: 'Martin usually shaves when he is in the BATHROOM'), the main clause restricts the domain of quantification. That is, in the first reading the adverb quantifies over situations when Martin is in the bathroom, while in the second reading it quantifies over situations when Martin shaves.

The fact that preposed *when*-clauses are unambiguous, while postponed *when*-clauses can have two different interpretations, suggests that the same considerations which played a role in the determination of temporal anaphorization also determine the argument structure of adverbial quantification. Crucially, the rhetorical structure of the *when*-clause construction is embedded under quantification. Consequently, we expect both TA and DOAP-R to be relevant constraints. However, the situation is slightly more complex, because we have to establish a connection between the quantificational and the rhetorical structure. What we see is that the argument structure of the quantificational relation reflects the antecedent-anaphor order of the rhetorical relation. This suggests an extension of the $\alpha\beta$ constraint. The new formulation of this constraint is spelled out in (61):

(61) $\alpha\beta$: The linear order of two clauses corresponds to the order antecedent-anaphor in a rhetorical structure, which corresponds to the order restrictor-scope in a quantificational structure, i.e., $\alpha\beta$: $R(\alpha,\beta)$: $Q(A,B)$.

The combination of TA, DOAP-R and the generalized version of αβ leads to the following tableau for preposed *when*-clauses embedded under an adverbial quantifier such as (60). A quantificational adverb denotes a relation between two sets of events. The first set of events can be given by either the *when*-clause or the main clause. The second argument is the set of these events further restricted by the events introduced by the other clause via a rhetorical relation between the two types of events. This embedding of a rhetorical relation in a quantificational structure results in six possible interpretations for a *when*-clause and main clause embedded under a quantificational adverb. Just like in the case of a preposed *when*-clause in a non-quantified sentence, we find one optimal candidate here which does not violate any constraints.

TABLEAU 7

The interpretation of a sentence containing an adverbial quantifier and a preposed *when*-clause

Adverb [*when*-clause (e_1); main clause (e_2)]	TA	DOAP-R	αβ
☞ $Q(E_1, \{e_1: \exists e_2\, R(e_1, e_2)\})$			
$Q(E_1, \{e_1: \exists e_2\, R(e_2, e_1)\})$	*!		**
$Q(E_1, \{e_1: \exists e_2\, \neg R\})$		*!	
$Q(E_2, \{e_2: \exists e_1\, R(e_1, e_2)\})$			*!
$Q(E_2, \{e_2: \exists e_1\, R(e_2, e_1)\})$	*!		*
$Q(E_2, \{e_2: \exists e_1\, \neg R\})$		*!	*

The output candidates are quantifiers, relating two argument sets of eventualities, for example the set of events given by e_1 and the set of events e_1 that are further restricted by a second event e_2 that is or is not in a rhetorical relation with e_1. As in the cases of unembedded temporal anaphorization, we observe that the combination of the three constraints yields the desired interpretation. For (60), this is the interpretation in which all events in which Martin would be in the bathroom provide the antecedent for, and thus temporally include the events in which he would shave. That means that so far we can maintain the ranking proposed for the unembedded *when*-clauses. In order to explore the explanatory power of these constraints further, we need to consider postponed *when*-clauses under quantification. Consider next the tableau for inputs such as (59).

TABLEAU 8
The interpretation of a sentence containing an adverbial quantifier and a
postponed *when*-clause

Adverb [main clause (e_2); *when*-clause (e_1)]	TA	DOAP-R	$\alpha\beta$
☞ $Q(E_1, \{e_1: \exists e_2\ R(e_1, e_2)\})$			*
$Q(E_1, \{e_1: \exists e_2\ R(e_2, e_1)\})$	*!		*
$Q(E_1, \{e_1: \exists e_2\ \neg R\})$		*	*!
$Q(E_2, \{e_2: \exists e_1\ R(e_1, e_2)\})$			**!
$Q(E_2, \{e_2: \exists e_1\ R(e_2, e_1)\})$	*!		
☞ $Q(E_2, \{e_2: \exists e_1\ \neg R\})$		*	

Two candidates emerge as optimal interpretations. The first one violates $\alpha\beta$, and treats the postponed *when*-clause as the antecedent of the rhetorical structure. The generalized version of $\alpha\beta$ requires the quantificational structure to reflect the rhetorical structure. Corresponding to the syntactic order but not to the rhetorical structure thus leads to two violations of $\alpha\beta$ (as in the fourth candidate in the tableau). The second possible interpretation satisfies $\alpha\beta$, but it violates DOAP-R. In the absence of a rhetorical relation between the two clauses, the quantificational structure corresponds to syntactic structure directly. That is, the quantifier takes the first clause as its first argument, and the second clause as its second argument. This leads to quantification over the set of events provided by the main clause in (59).[4]

Just like in the case of unembedded temporal anaphorization, we observe that the two optimal candidates for sentences with postponed *when*-clauses each violate one constraint. This suggests that our initial hypothesis that DOAP-R and $\alpha\beta$ are ranked equally high is confirmed by the quantificational case. Note that an interpretation in which TA is violated remains unavailable. This confirms our claim that TA is ranked higher than the other two conditions. We conclude that the same constraints which play a role in temporal anaphorization govern the interpretation of *when*-clause constructions under quantification. The result is a small set of constraints which al-

---

[4] De Hoop and de Swart (2000) account for the fact that the two readings correlate with a particular topic-focus structure. However, they also show that topic-focus structure *follows* syntactic and rhetorical structure, rather than being a direct trigger of a particular interpretation. This is in accordance with the fact that for preposed *when*-clauses only one interpretation is available, independently of the role of focus.

lows just the right amount of flexibility in the interpretation of these sentences. Crucially, the constraints are cross-modular, and involve a mix of syntactic, semantic, and pragmatic information.

3.4 Compositionality and Bidirectionality

Reconsider the sentences (12) and (13) discussed in Section 3.3.1 above, repeated below.

(62) Most people drink at night.

(63) Most people sleep at night.

We argued that although the syntactic structures of these two sentences are absolutely identical, the preferred (default) interpretations differ truth-conditionally. The preferred reading of the first sentence can be paraphrased as 'When it is night, most people sleep' whereas the preferred reading of the second sentence is not 'When it is night, most people drink' but rather, 'When people drink, mostly it is at night'.

As we pointed out in Section 3.3.1 above, it is not so easy to formalize the influence of context and lexical knowledge on the truth-conditional differences between the two sentences. The reason is that different factors may be in conflict with each other. That is, syntactic structure, lexical material, context, and world knowledge may all help in arriving at the correct interpretation of sentences such as *Most people drink at night*. But crucially, these different factors do not just function one after the other as reducers of the presumably infinite set of interpretations given by a highly underspecified representation. In fact, the different factors can be *in conflict*.

For example, the lexical meaning of *most* gives us the relation between two sets such that the intersection contains more elements than the difference between the two does. The lexical material within the sentence and the syntactic structure of the sentence give us these two sets, in this case, the set of people and the set of individuals that drink at night. This would give us the optimal (hence, preferred) interpretation in the absence of further context, and in fact, that would give us the optimal interpretation in the case of *Most people sleep at night*.

For the sentence *Most people drink at night*, however, this interpretation gives rise to a conflict with our world knowledge. As it is probably not even true that most people drink (where *drink* is generally understood as *drink alcohol*), it is hard to believe that it holds for most people that they drink at night. So, there is a conflict between the information provided by the syntactic structure of the sentence and the information provided by our world knowledge. This conflict is resolved by considering the next optimal interpretation (that is, 'next optimal' purely on the basis of the syntactic structure of the sentence). This is the interpretation such that the set of people gets intersected with the generalized union over the set of alternatives for a certain constituent in the sentence.

If intonational information is available, then the constituent that gives rise to this set of alternatives is the syntactic argument containing the focus (where focus is marked by sentential accent). In the absence of intonation, we may consider what would be the unmarked constituent to bear the focus. In the case of *Most people drink at night*, the default position of the sentential accent seems to be on *at night*. This gives us as a domain of quantification of *most* the set of people who drink (at certain times). Hence, the interpretation for the entire sentence is that for most of the people who drink (alcohol) it holds that they drink at night. This interpretation is not in conflict with our world knowledge, and it is in fact the optimal (that is, preferred) interpretation against an empty context.

Of course, in the presence of an actual context, another interpretation might become optimal. So, the sentence *Most people DRINK at night* might be used as an answer to the question why there are so many empty beds in the middle of the night, with a concomitant interpretation. Again, this interpretation would deviate from the interpretation dictated by the syntactic structure of the sentence alone.

In these cases, in the competition between a syntactically optimal but pragmatically unlikely interpretation and a pragmatically optimal but syntactically suboptimal interpretation, the latter wins. The advantage of an optimization approach to interpretation is clearly that it can deal with actual conflicts among different factors.

Let us relate this to the principle of recoverability, extensively discussed in Chapter 2: Only elements whose semantic content can be recovered from the local context may be left unpronounced. If a speaker wishes to express the meaning that most linguists drink, and if the topic of the discourse is linguists, then the speaker may utter the sentence *Most drink*. A hearer will then be able to infer that the missing noun must be interpreted as the set of linguists. On the other hand, if the topic of the discourse is some other entity, for example people present at the conference, and if the speaker again wishes to express the meaning that most linguists drink, then she cannot leave the noun unpronounced. If the speaker would utter the sentence *Most drink* in this context, the hearer would mistakenly interpret the missing noun as the set of people present at the conference.

Recoverability is usually assumed to be a meta-restriction on syntactic analyses. However, its status appears to be similar to the status of the principle of compositionality in semantics. Compositionality is crucial to a hearer who wishes to interpret a certain utterance. She must use all, possibly conflicting, information to arrive at the intended meaning of this utterance. Importantly from the perspective of bidirectional OT, the hearer must also take into account all options and information available to a speaker. Similarly, recoverability is crucial to a speaker who wishes to express a certain meaning. She must use all information to arrive at a certain form for this meaning. Again, the speaker must also take into account the way a hearer would interpret the sentence.

So compositionality and recoverability appear to be two sides of the same coin. While compositionality relates to the task of the hearer, recoverability relates to the task of the speaker. Both principles require that the perspective of the other conversational partner is also taken into account. We therefore propose to view compositionality problems in the light of bidirectional optimization. Indeed, bidirectional OT guarantees a general procedure of optimization from form to meaning and from meaning to form. In effect, the communication between the speaker and the hearer thus proceeds in an optimal way.

At this point, we wish to broaden our concept of compositionality to what Van Gelder (1990) has dubbed **functional compositionality**. Van Gelder (1990) distinguishes between concatenative and functional compositionality. He describes the essence of a concatenative mode of combination informally as 'a way of *linking* or *ordering* successive constituents without altering them in any way as it forms the compound expression.' For example, tokens of the symbol 'P' are the same whether appearing standing alone, P, or in the context of an expression such as *(P&Q)*. Obviously, the thesis of context independency is based on this type of compositionality (cf. Hintikka 1983, cited in Janssen 1997): 'The meaning of an expression should not depend on the context in which it occurs.' Yet, although formal languages of mathematics, logic, and computer science are all compositional in this concatenative sense, concatenation is not the only way of implementing the combination of elements in getting a compound expression. Van Gelder (1990) points out that functional compositionality can be obtained whenever there are general, effective, and reliable processes for (a) producing an expression given its constituents, and (b) decomposing the expression back into those constituents. Whereas concatenative schemes are always functionally compositional as well, it is possible to have merely functionally compositional schemes that are *not* concatenative. One of the key principles in formal approaches to natural language interpretation is the principle of compositionality, which expresses the idea that the meaning of a complex expression can be derived from the meanings of its parts and the way these parts are syntactically linked. Smolensky (1995) notes that 'It would constitute significant progress to be able to reduce the (symbolic) principle of semantic compositionality to more basic connectionist principles (...) Developing such a connectionist semantics might well involve formalizing the weak notion of compositionality.' With *weak compositionality* Smolensky refers to compositionality in an 'approximate' sense: a non-concatenative way of combining contextually dependent (representations of) elements of a compound expression. In that sense, Smolensky's weak compositionality is reminiscent to Frege's (1884) contextuality principle, cited in Janssen (1997): 'A word has a meaning only in the context of a sentence, not in separation.'

Connectionist models are often criticized for their lack of compositionality, since interpretation is assigned to activity patterns but not to individual units. But as Van Gelder (1990) points out, 'The absence of strictly syntactic structure, however, does not imply the absence of significant structure of any kind.' Connectionist approaches to language, such as bidirectional optimization, provide the necessary tools to combine different pieces of information (from context, world knowledge, lexicon, syntax) in a precisely defined way, by evaluating form-meaning pairs against a set of ranked (cross-modular) constraints. Bidirectional OT thus provides a general, effective, and reliable process for producing and comprehending complex expressions, therefore it *is* compositional in Van Gelder's sense (i.e. composing and decomposing of complex expressions in a nontrivial and independent way). Although this type of compositionality is broader than the classical conception of compositionality, it is nevertheless in accordance with the hypothesis of **direct compositionality**, in that there is a direct mapping from form to meaning in the process of bidirectional optimization of form-meaning pairs.

Bidirectional Optimality Theory provides the necessary tools to combine different pieces of information (from context, world knowledge, lexicon, syntax) in a precisely defined way. Information provided by the meaning of the lexical items or the syntactic structure can interact or even compete with information given by the context. But in each case the optimal solution should be predictable as the different constraints are ranked with respect to each other. Thus, within OT the interpretation of a complex expression is brought out by an optimization procedure that takes into account syntactic and contextual information simultaneously on the basis of a ranked set of constraints of various nature.

Bidirectional OT adds to this general procedure that the hearer takes into account the speaker perspective (and, the other way around, that the speaker takes into account the hearer perspective). That is, if a form is associated with a certain interpretation within a certain context by a hearer, then within that same context, the same meaning would have been expressed by the same form if the hearer would have been the speaker. To put it differently, the composition of a form-meaning pair within a context goes hand in hand with the decomposition of that form-meaning pair within that same context.

By evaluating form-meaning pairs against a set of ranked (cross-modular) constraints, bidirectional OT thus guarantees a general procedure of optimization, which is functionally compositional in Van Gelder's (1990) sense. We conclude that compositionality can be maintained as an important principle in guiding the interpretation of a certain form within a certain context, but in a broader sense, such that lexical and syntactic information naturally interact with contextual sources of information. The main point is that bidirectional OT restricts interpretation in a way that is functionally compositional in the sense that composition and decomposition of a certain interpretation go hand in hand (Blutner, Hendriks, & de Hoop, 2003).

3.5 Scrambling Revisited: A Bidirectional OT Analysis

In the second section of this chapter we considered the scrambling behavior of definites in Dutch. Definite noun phrases can have anaphoric and non-anaphoric readings and we showed that although there is a tendency for anaphoric definites to scramble (that is, to occupy the position to the left of the adverb), this is by no means obligatory. In fact, both anaphoric and non-anaphoric noun phrases can occur either to the left or to the right of a sentential adverb. This freedom in word order was accounted for by an OT syntactic analysis. At the same time, we set up an OT semantic analysis with two constraints, NEW and DOAP, and argued that the proposed ranking DOAP » NEW is sufficient to explain the fact that an anaphoric interpretation for a definite NP is optimal whenever there is a suitable antecedent in the discourse, and independent of the position (scrambled or unscrambled) of the definite noun phrase.

However, we concluded the second section by pointing out that this type of analysis would not be able to account for the scrambling behavior of indefinites and pronouns. In the present section we will argue that in order to account for the scrambling phenomena involving indefinites and pronouns in Dutch, we must assume a bidirectional OT perspective.

Reconsider the basic facts. In Dutch, indefinite noun phrases do not like to scramble: indefinite noun phrases in scrambled position sometimes even give rise to ill-formedness (van der Does & de Hoop, 1998). But when they do scramble, there is a concomitant 'special effect', that is, a shift in meaning.

(64) Paul zei dat   hij   gisteren   een boek heeft gelezen.
      Paul said that   he   yesterday   a   book has   read
      'Paul said that he read a book yesterday.'

(65) Paul zei dat   hij   een boek gisteren   heeft gelezen.
      Paul said that   he   a   book yesterday   has   read
      'Paul said that he read a book yesterday.'

The preferred reading of the unscrambled indefinite object in (64) is the non-referential reading which is indeed the unmarked (i.e. most frequent) meaning for indefinite objects. In contrast, the scrambled indefinite object in (65) receives a referential ('specific') reading. The unmarked (most frequent) position for indefinite objects is the unscrambled position. When an indefinite object ends up in the marked (scrambled) position, this gives rise to a shift in meaning. In (65), the indefinite object gets a referential reading, which may indeed be considered a marked (less frequent) meaning of an indefinite object. Note that other 'marked' meanings happen to exist as well, such as 'generic', or 'contrastively focused' readings, dependent on the nature of the noun phrase, the adverb and the context (cf. de Hoop, 1996).

The scrambled position is not the marked (less frequent) position for all objects. Pronouns usually scramble, so for pronouns the word order in (66) is the unmarked one.

(66) Paul   zei   dat   hij   haar   gisteren   heeft   gezien.
      Paul   said   that   he   her   yesterday has   seen
      'Paul said that he saw her yesterday.'

(67) Paul   zei   dat   hij   gisteren   haar   heeft   gezien.
      Paul   said   that   he   yesterday her   has   seen
      'Paul said that he saw HER yesterday.'

The unmarked reading that goes with the unmarked (scrambled) position of the pronominal object in (66) is the anaphoric reading. When the pronoun occupies the marked (unscrambled) position, this induces a shift in meaning. The reading that arises for the pronoun in the unscrambled position in (67) is a deictic (i.e. non-anaphoric) reading, which is indeed a marked (less frequent) meaning for pronouns. It is naturally obtained when the speaker stresses the pronoun, preferably accompanied by a movement of the head towards a male individual or by pointing her finger at him. So, without further clues in the context from intonation, the unmarked order for the pronominal object in (66) is associated with an unmarked interpretation, that is, an anaphoric reading. In (67), however, the marked position induces a 'special effect', that is, a marked 'deictic' reading for the pronoun.

There is overwhelming evidence across languages that marked (less harmonic, less frequent, more complex) forms are used for marked (less harmonic, less frequent, more complex) meanings. This generalization is known as the markedness principle (Horn, 1984). Blutner (2000) notes that the markedness principle can be proven to result from (weak) bidirectional OT. We see that scrambling in Dutch obeys the principle of **markedness**, i.e., marked forms are used for marked meanings. For pronominal objects, this means that the unscrambled position is used for the deictic interpretation, while for indefinite objects, this means that the scrambled position is used for the referential interpretation.

The basic idea of bidirectional OT is to simultaneously optimize in both directions, from form to meaning and from meaning to form. As a consequence, bidirectional optimization involves the evaluation of form-meaning *pairs* against a set of ranked (cross-modular) constraints.

Instead of giving the relevant definitions of how to determine which pairs of forms and meanings are optimal, which will be postponed until Chapter 4, we will just provide a schematic example in order to illustrate the basic characteristics of bidirectional OT. Assume that we have two forms f_1 and f_2 and two meanings m_1 and m_2. We stipulate that the form f_1 is less marked (more harmonic) than the form f_2, which means that for a given meaning, form f_1 will be the optimal form. Furthermore, interpretation m_1 is less marked (more harmonic) than the interpretation m_2, which means that for a given form, meaning m_1 will be the optimal meaning. Thus, the following ordering relation between form-meaning pairs can be derived, represented in an arrow diagram, where the arrows point to the preferred pair.

(68) $<f_1, m_1>$ $\leftarrow$ $<f_2, m_1>$

$\uparrow$ $\qquad\qquad$ $\uparrow$

$<f_1, m_2>$ $\leftarrow$ $<f_2, m_2>$

In Blutner's (2000) framework a form-meaning pair $<f, m>$ is called **super-optimal** if and only if there is no other super-optimal pair $<f', m>$ such that $<f', m>$ is more harmonic than $<f, m>$ and there is no other super-optimal pair $<f, m'>$ such that $<f, m'>$ is more harmonic than $<f, m>$. The reader may verify that according to this definition, there are two super-optimal pairs in the diagram in (68), namely $<f_1, m_1>$ and $<f_2, m_2>$. Indeed, although f_2 is not an optimal form itself and m_2 is not an optimal meaning, the pair $<f_2, m_2>$ is super-optimal, because there is no super-optimal pair that blocks it (that is, the two candidates $<f_1, m_2>$ and $<f_2, m_1>$ are not super-optimal, because they are both blocked by the other super-optimal pair $<f_1$, $m_1>$).

Thus, bidirectional OT provides us with two super-optimal form-meaning pairs, in accordance with the markedness principle: the unmarked form with the unmarked meaning, and the marked form with the marked meaning.

Let us now give a bidirectional OT analysis of the data under discussion. We use the following four very simple and superficial constraints, dealing with the meaning and the form of indefinite objects and pronominal objects respectively. Of course, there are many approaches in the literature, which can offer more sophisticated constraints that would do the same job (dealing with information structure packaging, accentuation, etc.). However, for our present purposes we do not need any 'deeper explanations' for the data that we wish to explain.

(69) MEANING INDEFINITE OBJECT (MIO): An indefinite object gets a non-referential reading (presumably type <e,t>).

(70) FORM INDEFINITE OBJECT (FIO): An indefinite object does not scramble.

(71) MEANING OBJECT PRONOUN (MOP): A pronominal object gets an anaphoric reading.

(72) FORM OBJECT PRONOUN (FOP): A pronominal object scrambles.

The following two tableaux illustrate the four super-optimal pairs of form and meaning that we obtain using the above four constraints, indicated by the super-optimality sign '☝'.

TABLEAU 9
Super-optimal forms and meanings of indefinite objects

Indefinite object	FIO	MIO
☞ <[unscrambled], <e,t>>	✓	✓
<[scrambled], <e,t>>	*	✓
<[unscrambled], e>	✓	*
☞ <[scrambled], e>	*	*

TABLEAU 10
Super-optimal forms and meanings of pronominal objects

Pronominal object	FOP	MOP
☞ <[scrambled], 'anaphoric'>	✓	✓
<[unscrambled], 'anaphoric'>	*	✓
<[scrambled], 'deictic'>	✓	*
☞ <[unscrambled], 'deictic'>	*	*

To sum up, a bidirectional OT approach makes it possible to account for the fact that marked (sub-optimal) forms are used for marked (sub-optimal) meanings, in this case the use of the scrambled position for a referential indefinite object and the unscrambled position for a deictic pronominal object. Note that a bidirectional OT analysis was not necessary for the scrambling behavior of definite objects, analyzed in Section 3.2.1 above. This is due to the fact that definite objects are really in the middle between indefinites and pronouns with a rather free variation in position (scrambled or unscrambled) as well as meaning (anaphoric or non-anaphoric) and it would be hard to determine what would be the marked position and what would be the marked meaning in their case.

With respect to the scrambling behavior of indefinite and pronominal objects in Dutch, their unmarked forms and unmarked meanings would be the optimal outcomes of unidirectional optimization, either from form to meaning or *vice versa*. However, it is quite clear that a unidirectional approach (either productive or interpretive optimization) could never account for the occurrence of sub-optimal forms in combination with sub-optimal meanings in such a natural way. The pragmatic markedness principle captures these data very well and bidirectional OT straightforwardly accounts for this principle.

3.6 Summary

In this chapter we showed that OT semantics is able to account for the optionality in form but not in meaning of definite noun phrases in Dutch, as well as phenomena of anaphora and ellipsis resolution. We thus hope to have shown that OT semantics is a successful tool in characterizing natural language interpretation. Remaining problems related to the semantic principle of compositionality were solved by taking a bidirectional perspective on interpretation. In the last section, we concluded that scrambling data in Dutch provide a strong argument in favor of bidirectional OT. The next chapter is completely dedicated to this recent twist in the theory of optimization of interpretation.

4

Bidirectionality

4.1 Introduction

In this chapter we will demonstrate that the framework of OT semantics allows for an integration of pragmatic knowledge into semantic theory in a very straightforward fashion. The basic idea is to construct an inferential mechanism of utterance interpretation that conforms to the Gricean suggestion of conversational implicature. Using Johnson Laird's (1983) notion of a mental model we will relate this mechanism to the construction of mental models (Section 4.2). Next, we discuss some empirical peculiarities of the inferential mechanism. Section 4.3 discusses the non-monotonicity of invited inferences and Section 4.4 is devoted to the existence of (lexical) blocking. Exploiting ideas of Atlas and Levinson (1981) and Horn (1984), a straightforward formulation of conversational implicature is given in Section 4.5, and it is shown that this idea fits into a bidirectional OT framework. In Section 4.6 the effects of negative strengthening are analyzed within this framework.

4.2 Mental Models and Natural Language Interpretation

The important role that **mental models** play in natural language comprehension was clearly demonstrated by experimental psychologists in the 1970s (e.g. Johnson-Laird, 1981, 1983, 1988; Kintsch, 1974). Let us consider the following utterance:

(1) The tones sounded impure because the hem was torn.

Obviously, we do not really understand what this sentence means until we know that this sentence is about a bagpipe. It is evident that this difficulty is not due to our insufficient knowledge of English. The syntax involved is quite simple and there are no unknown words in the sentence. Instead, the difficulty is related to trouble in accessing the relevant conceptual setting. The idea of bagpiping is simply too unexpected to be derived in a quasi-neutral utterance context. The example demonstrates that we have to distinguish carefully between the linguistic aspects of representing the (formal) meaning of sentences and the pragmatic aspects of utterance interpretation. The latter is enriching the former. The construction of a vivid mental model yields much more information than that provided by the semantically coded truth conditions.

Another classical example is due to an experiment by Bransford, Barklay, and Franks (1982). These authors confronted subjects with study sentences like (2) and tested them on sentences like (3):

(2)   Three turtles rested *beside/on* a floating log, and a fish swam beneath *them.*

(3)   Three turtles rested *beside/on* a floating log, and a fish swam beneath *it.*

When the preposition is *on*, (2) easily implies (3) based on world knowledge and the ability of spatial reasoning. But when it is *beside*, the implication does not go through. The important finding was that errors in recognition favored (3) only when the preposition was *on*. In this case, the subjects tend to confuse (2) with (3) since both utterances express the same spatial situation. The conclusion was that memory in a normal situation is not really memory for 'meaning'. Rather, it is memory for the products of comprehension, including visual imagery of the scenic or situational objects and including characteristics and relative relationships among the objects described in the discourse. Mental models and other global representational means (cf. Clark & Clark, 1977) are an appropriate representational instrument to express the products of comprehension.

Considerations of this kind demonstrate the distinction between semantics proper and pragmatic-contextual mechanisms of conceptual reconstruction. Taking this distinction as an important one, we are concerned with two different types of mechanisms:

(i)   A pragmasemantic mechanism that deals with the combinatorial aspects of meaning. This interpretive mechanism is allowed to include parts of contextual information if this is required to determine the **truth-conditional content** of the utterance under discussion (see Chapter 3).

(ii)   A pragmatic mechanism that deals with conceptual enrichment and reconstruction (= the construction of mental models). The architecture of the bidirectional OT system presented in Chapter 1 (Figure 2) relates this mechanism to the **conceptual system**, which builds on the semantic outcome of the OT grammar.

For Grice (1975) the theoretical distinction between what the speaker explicitly said and what she has merely implicated is of particular importance. What has been said is supposed to be based purely on the conventional meaning of a sentence, and is the subject of semantics. What is implicitly conveyed (**scalar and conversational implicatures**) belongs to the realm of pragmatics. It is assumed to be calculable on the basis of contextual information. Fruitful as this theoretical division of labor may have been, especially as a demarcation of the task of logical semantics, it has inherent problems. More often than not, what is said by a speaker's use of a sentence already depends on the context. Even for Griceans, propositional content is not fully fleshed out until reference, tense, and other indexical elements are fixed. However, propositional content must be *inferred* in many cases, going beyond the simple mechanism of fixing indexical elements.

Proponents of relevance theory (see, for example, Carston, 2002, 2003, 2004; Sperber & Wilson, 1986) have pointed out that the pragmatic reasoning used to compute implicated meaning (called implicature) must also be invoked to find out the relevant propositions where the formal meaning contributed by the linguistic expression itself is insufficient to give a proper account of truth-conditional content. Hence, relevance theory is assuming a Gricean mechanism of pragmatic strengthening in two different ways. First, it is used in order to fill the gap between formal, linguistic meaning and the propositional content (i.e., the *explicit* assumptions communicated by an utterance). This is called **explicature** in relevance theory (cf. Sperber & Wilson, 1986). Second, it is used to calculate what relevance theoreticians call **implicature**.

One example from Carston (2004) can help to clarify the explicature/implicature distinction.

(4)   X: How is Mary feeling after her first year at university?
      Y: She didn't get enough units and can't continue.

Suppose that, in the particular context, X takes Y to have communicated the following assumptions:

(5) a. MARY$_x$ DID NOT PASS ENOUGH UNIVERSITY COURSE UNITS TO QUALIFY FOR ADMISSION TO SECOND YEAR STUDY AND, AS A RESULT, MARY$_x$ CANNOT CONTINUE WITH UNIVERSITY STUDY.
b. MARY$_x$ IS NOT FEELING VERY HAPPY.[1]

The proposition (5a) is intended to express an explicature of Y's utterance in (4), and (5b) may be taken to express an implicature. The latter proposition refers to an independent assumption, inferred as a whole from the former proposition.[2] Obviously, the calculation of implicature goes beyond the truth conditional content of an utterance and will be related here to the construction of mental models. At this point we should stress that bidirectional OT proves to be a useful research instrument for the analysis of both explicature and implicature.

Concluding, the present view does not completely conform to a Gricean perspective. It fits much better to the framework of **relevance theory** (Sperber & Wilson, 1986). Chapter 3 was concerned with examples that conform to the relevance theoretic notion of explicature. For example, the difference in interpretation between *Most people drink at night* and *Most people sleep at night* (examples (12) and (13) of Chapter 3) clearly conforms to a difference in the respective explicatures, since the propositional content of the two sentences is different. For the first sentence a paraphrase of the propositional content is 'Most people who drink, drink at night', and for the second it is 'At night, most people sleep'. Though it is not always simple to draw the precise boundaries between explicature and implicature, we take the difference as a very important one, since it conforms to two different mechanisms of enrichment. In the first case, the enrichment has to do with restricting some relevant parameters in the underlying semantic representations, for example by restricting the domain of quantification. In the second case it refers to the construction of explicit, mental models. The present chapter will throw some light on the second kind of mechanism, dealing with the notion of implicature via the optimization of mental models.

---

[1] Small capitals are used to distinguish propositions from natural language sentences; the subscripted x indicates that a particular referent has been assigned to the name 'Mary'.

[2] Note that without the question/context (4X), (4Y) would not give rise to the implicature in (5b).

4.3 The Non-Monotonicity of Invited Inferences

It was the evident divergence between the formal devices $\neg$, $\wedge$, $\vee$, $\supset$, $(\forall x)$, $(\exists x)$ (in their standard two-valued interpretation) and their natural language counterparts that was the starting point of Grice's 'logic of conversation' (Grice, 1989). In subsequent work these divergences were investigated carefully from an empirical and a theoretical point of view, sometimes adopting Grice's conceptual framework and sometimes rejecting it. For example, Geis and Zwicky (1971) introduced and discussed the inference scheme they dubbed **conditional perfection**, the notorious tendency to 'perfect' an *if* conditional into the corresponding biconditional (*if and only if*, *iff*). As an example, the utterance of (6a) was claimed to invite the inference of (6b), thus conveying the utterance meaning of (6c).

(6) a. If you mow the lawn, I'll give you $5.
     b. If you don't mow the lawn, I won't give you $5.
     c. If and only if you mow the lawn, I'll give you $5.

In order to account for such inferences, it may be appealing to use rules in the style of natural deduction. For example, we could introduce an inference rule like the following:

(7) $\underline{\text{if } (p, q)}$
        $\therefore$ if($\neg$p, $\neg$q)

Obviously, (7) can be seen as instantiating the inference from (6a) to (6b). However, in contrast to inference rules like Modus Ponens or Simplification, the structure-sensitivity of which is never violated, the same does not hold for the schema (7). This was demonstrated by many authors (for a recent survey cf. Horn, 2000). The following example shows a situation where the corresponding inferences cannot be drawn:

(8) a. If you're in Toronto, you are in Canada.
     b. If you're not in Toronto, you're not in Canada.
     c. If and only if you're in Toronto, you are in Canada.

There are at least three different strategies of dealing with this observation. The first one is to assume a lexical ambiguity of *if* stipulating two readings: the standard reading and the biconditional reading. The second strategy is to doubt that the tendency of drawing invited inferences in the sense of Geis and Zwicky is a real one, and it aims to reduce the relevant observation exclusively to language-independent factors. The third strategy accepts the reality of these inferences, and, at the same time, acknowledges the non-monotonicity of (parts of) our inferential competence. After pointing out that all three strategies are represented in the literature, Horn (2000) demonstrates that the third strategy is the most promising one. What's more, he suggests to clarify the strategy in terms of a non-monotonic operation of pragmatic strengthening[3], a suggestion we want to follow in the theoretical part of this chapter.

Negation in natural language is a rich source of a variety of non-logical inferences (see Horn, 1989). Standard examples are **scalar implicatures** (*Not all of the students came* ≈> *Some of them came*). Others are collected under the term **negative strengthening**.[4] The latter are concerned with the effect of preferred interpretations that occurs when certain sentence types are negated.

One instance of the phenomenon of negative strengthening arises in connection with gradable adjectives typically occurring as antonyms, such as {*good, bad*}, {*large, small*}, {*happy, unhappy*}. Semantically, the elements of antonym pairs are **contraries**, that is, they are mutually inconsistent but do not exhaust the whole spectrum, permitting a non-empty middle ground.

What are the effects of negating gradable adjectives? For the sake of explicitness let us consider the gradable antonyms *happy* and *unhappy*, and assume three possible states of happiness, iconized by ☺, ☹, and ☻. These states function as mental models of situations expressing graded evaluations. Not unexpectedly, we want to take *happy* as referring to the first state, *unhappy* as referring to the second state, and *neither happy nor unhappy* as referring to the third state.

Let us consider first the effect of negating positive adjectives, starting with a sentence like (9a). Obviously, the preferred interpretation of this sentence is (9c); this corresponds to a logical strengthening of the content of (9a) which is paraphrased in (9b). The discourse (9d) shows that the effect of strengthening (9c) is defeasible. This indicates that the inferential notion that underlies the phenomenon of strengthening ought to be non-monotonic.

(9) a. I'm not happy.
    b. It isn't the case that I'm happy.   (*Entailment*)   ☹ ☻

---

[3] This contrasts with the view of Geis and Zwicky (1971) who insist that their 'invited inferences' are notably different from 'conversational implicatures' in the sense of Grice.
[4] For discussions of the phenomenon of negative strengthening see Horn (1989) and Levinson (2000).

   c. I'm unhappy.   (*Implicature*)   ☹
   d. I'm not happy and not unhappy.   (*Defeasibility*)

Following Levinson (2000), the effect of negative strengthening for positive adjectives can be illustrated in the following way:

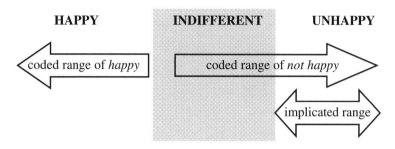

Figure 1   Negative strengthening as implicated contraries

It describes the effect of negative strengthening as implicating contraries from contradictions.

    The illustrated shape of negative strengthening is restricted to the positive (unmarked) element of an antonym pair. When considering negative adjectives, deviations from this pattern may be found. The deviations are rather obvious for adjectives with incorporated affixal negation. This leads us to the well-known case of double negation (**litotes**):

(10) a. I'm not unhappy.
    b. It isn't the case that I'm unhappy.   (*Entailment*)   ☺ ☻
    c. I'm neither happy nor unhappy.   (*Implicature*)   ☻
    d. I'm rather happy   (*Proper Implicature*)
       (but not quite as happy as using the expression *happy* would suggest).
    e. I'm not unhappy, in fact I'm happy.   (*Defeasibility*)

Admitting only three states on the happiness scale allows only a rather rough approximation of the interpretive effects. The simplest approximation describes negative strengthening as a preference for the middle ground. This is what (10c) expresses. A more appropriate formulation of the effect is given in (10d). For the sake of precision, we had to introduce an intermediate state between ☺ and ☻ (on the scale of happiness). In the following diagram a more adequate illustration of the basic pattern is presented (as described in Horn, 1984; Levinson, 2000).

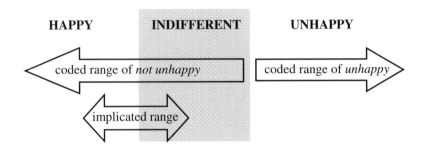

Figure 2   Litotes: When two negatives do not make a positive

As in the case discussed before, the effect of negative strengthening proves defeasible, a fact that requires the underlying mechanism to be non-monotonic.

The theoretical discussion of the phenomenon of negative strengthening is postponed until Section 4.5 and 4.6, where the ideas of Horn and Levinson will be outlined and a formal account of their ideas will be given in terms of Optimality Theory.

4.4 Blocking

Another general problem that (lexical) semantics has to address is the phenomenon of **lexical blocking**. This phenomenon has been demonstrated in a number of examples where the appropriate use of a given expression formed by a relatively productive process is restricted by the existence of a more 'lexicalized' alternative to this expression. One case in point was provided by Householder (1971). The adjective *pale* can be combined with a great many color words: *pale green, pale blue, pale yellow*. However, the combination *pale red* is limited in a way that the other combinations are not. For some speakers *pale red* is simply anomalous, and for others it picks up whatever part of the pale domain of red *pink* has not preempted. This suggests that the combinability of *pale* is fully or partially blocked by the lexical alternative *pink*.

Another standard example is the phenomenon of blocking in the context of derivational and inflectional morphological processes. Aronoff (1976) has shown that the existence of a simple lexical item can block the formation of an otherwise expected affixally derived form synonymous with it. In particular, the existence of a simple abstract nominal underlying a given *-ous* adjective blocks its nominalization with *-ity*:

(11) a. curious – curiosity; tenacious – tenacity
   b. furious - *furiosity – fury; fallacious - *fallacity - fallacy

While Aronoff's formulation of blocking was limited to derivational processes, Kiparsky (1983) notes that blocking may also extend to inflectional processes and he suggests a reformulation of Aronoff's blocking as a subcase of the Elsewhere Condition: special rules block general rules in their shared domain. However, Kiparsky cites examples of **partial blocking** in order to show that this formulation is too strong. According to Kiparsky, partial blocking corresponds to the phenomenon that the special (less productive) affix occurs in some restricted meaning and the general (more productive) affix picks up the remaining meaning (consider examples like *refrigerant - refrigerator, informant - informer, contestant - contester*). To handle these and other cases, Kiparsky (1983) formulates a general condition which he calls Avoid Synonymy: 'The output of a lexical rule may not be synonymous with an existing lexical item'.

Working independently of the Aronoff-Kiparsky line, McCawley (1978) collects a number of further examples demonstrating the phenomenon of partial blocking outside the domain of derivational and inflectional processes. For example, he observes that the distribution of productive causatives (in English, Japanese, German, and other languages) is restricted by the existence of a corresponding lexical causative. Whereas lexical causatives (e.g. (12a)) tend to be restricted in their distribution to the stereotypical causative situation (direct, unmediated causation through physical action), productive (periphrastic) causatives tend to pick up more marked situations of mediated, indirect causation. For example, (12b) could be used appropriately when Black Bart caused the sheriff's gun to backfire by stuffing it with cotton.

(12) a. Black Bart killed the sheriff.
   b. Black Bart caused the sheriff to die.

The phenomenon of blocking can be taken as evidence demonstrating the apparent non-monotonicity of the lexical system. This becomes pretty clear when we take an ontogenetic perspective on the development of the lexical system. Children overgeneralize at some stage while developing their lexical system. For example, they acquire the productive rule of deriving deverbal adjectives with *-able* and apply this rule to produce *washable, breakable,* *readable*, but also *seeable* and *hearable*. Only later, after paired forms like *seeable/visible* and *hearable/audible* have coexisted for a while, will the meanings of the specialized items block the regularly derived forms. Examples of this kind suggest that the development of word meanings cannot be described as a process of accumulating more and more denotational knowledge in a monotonic way. Instead, there are highly non-monotonic stages in lexical development. At the moment, it is not clear whether this ontogenetic feature must be reflected in the logical structure of the mental lexicon. Rather, it is possible that pragmatic factors (such as Gricean rules of conversation) play an important role in determining which possible words are actual and what they really denote (Dowty, 1979; Horn, 1984; McCawley, 1978)

4.5 Conversational Implicature, Pragmatic Strengthening and Bidirectional OT

In the late 70s a renewed interest in the formal treatment of indexical expressions (*I, you, he, here, now, that, that book,* etc.) within model-theoretic semantics can be observed, inspired primarily by the work of Montague (e.g. Montague, 1970). The basic idea was to fill in some of the gaps in earlier work by Carnap and others by introducing aspects of context into formal semantics. As a result of these efforts, something like a classical theory of context-dependency originated.[5]

The classical view sees content being fully determined by linguistic meaning relative to a contextual index. In contrast, there is the so-called 'radical pragmatics' school (see, for instance, Cole, 1981). The radical view takes it that, although linguistic meaning is clearly important to content, it does not determine it, as pragmatic principles also play a role. The central issue of this approach is how to give a principled account of the determination of content. Seeing linguistic meanings as underdetermining the content (proposition) expressed, there must be a pragmatic mechanism of completion which can be best represented as an optimization procedure.

The school of 'radical pragmatics' does not make the distinction between explicature and implicature, and from the perspective of the basically Gricean mechanism of pragmatic strengthening this distinction does not seem to be critical. However, we think there are crucial representational differences which relate to the overall organization of the different cognitive subsystems (see Chapter 1). Calculating explicatures involves the interpre-

---

[5] In this place, it is not even possible to give a rough outline of this theory. Therefore, we refer to the original literature, e.g. Kaplan (1979).

tive component of the bidirectional OT grammar; calculating implicatures relates to the construction of mental models (conceptual system). Another aspect of discrimination has to do with the distinction between precisification and specification (Pinkal, 1995). In everyday speech, it is not uncommon to hear someone say (a) *Could you be more precise?* or (b) *Could you be more specific?*. In the first case the addressee is asked to avoid ambiguity and/or to be less vague. In the second case he simply should be more concrete. For example, it often happens that some categories need further specification in naming the finer distinctions which identify the referent. We see explicature as a mechanism related to precisification and implicature as one related to specification.

For Griceans, conversational implicatures are those non-truth-functional aspects of utterance interpretation which are conveyed by virtue of the assumption that the speaker and the hearer are obeying the **cooperative principle** of conversation, and, more specifically, various **conversational maxims** of quantity, quality, relation, and manner. While the notion of conversational implicature does not seem hard to grasp intuitively, it has proven difficult to define precisely. An important step in reducing and explicating the Gricean framework has been made by Atlas and Levinson (1981) and Horn (1984). Taking Quantity as starting point they distinguish between two principles, the Q-principle and the I-principle (termed the R-principle by Horn, 1984). Simple informal formulations of these principles are as follows:

(13) **Q-principle**

- Say as much as you can (given I) (Horn, 1984: 13).
- Make your contribution as informative (strong) as possible (Matsumoto, 1995: 23).
- Do not provide a statement that is informationally weaker than your knowledge of the world allows, unless providing a stronger statement would contravene the I-principle (Levinson, 1987: 401).

(14) **I-principle**

- Don't say more than you must (given Q) (Horn, 1984: 13).
- Say as little as necessary, i.e., produce the minimal linguistic information sufficient to achieve your communicational ends (bearing the Q-principle in mind) (Levinson, 1987: 402).
- Read as much into an utterance as is consistent with what you know about the world (Levinson, 1983: 146-47).

Obviously, the Q-principle corresponds to the first part of Grice's quantity maxim (*Make your contribution as informative as required*), while it can be argued that the countervailing I-principle collects the second part of the quantity maxim (*Do not make your contribution more informative than is required*), the maxim of relation and at least two of the manner submaxims, *Be brief* and *Be orderly*. As Horn (1984) seeks to demonstrate, the two principles can be seen as representing two competing forces, one force of unification minimizing the speaker's effort (I-principle), and one force of diversification minimizing the hearer's effort (Q-principle).

Conversational implicatures which are derivable essentially by appeal to the Q-principle are called Q-based implicatures. Standard examples are scalar implicatures and clausal implicatures. I-based implicatures, derivable essentially by appeal to the I-principle, can be generally characterized as enriching what is said via inference to a rich, stereotypical interpretation (cf. Gazdar, 1979; Atlas & Levinson, 1981; Horn, 1984; Levinson, 2000).

The proper treatment of conversational implicature crucially depends on the proper formulation of the Q- and the I-principle. The present explication which relates to Blutner (1998) in crucial aspects rests on the assumption that the semantic description of an utterance *f* is determining a range of possible mental models (or mental enrichments) *m*, one of which covers the intended situational content. There are different possibilities to make explicit what possible mental models/enrichments are: the idea of abductive specification may be useful (e.g. Hobbs et al., 1993), and likewise the idea of non-monotonic unification (e.g. Lascarides et al., 1995). Both mechanisms make use of the notion of common ground, which informally can be introduced as an information state containing all the propositions shared by several participants, including general world and discourse knowledge. We will not be very specific about the device that generates possible mental models. Besides the two mentioned approaches the model theoretic conceptions in general and Zeevat's (1998) idea of updating the common ground in particular can be used as alternatives. For the sake of convenience, we simply assume a function GEN that determines for each common ground σ what the possible mental models/enrichments of f are. In other words,

(15) $<f, m>$ is called a **possible enrichment pair** iff $<f, m> \in GEN_\sigma$, i.e., m can be generated from f by means of a common ground σ.

The other important part of OT that is necessary to reconstruct the essence of conversational implicature is the EVAL component. This component evaluates possible enrichment pairs and can be seen as being defined by a cost function $\underline{c}(f, m)$ in the general case. For example, in weighted abduction (Hobbs et al., 1993) this function reflects the proof cost for deriving a mental model/enrichment m from the underlying form f.[6] For the present aims it is not necessary to have the numerical values of this cost function. What is sufficient is an **ordering relation** $\prec$ *(being less costly, being more economical, being more harmonic)* defined on the possible enrichment pairs.[7] To be sure, the concrete realization of this ordering relation relates to a variety of different graded factors such as informativity, relevance, and effort, and is a matter for empirical investigation (cf. Ducrot, 1972; cf. Merin, 1999; van Rooy, 2004).

In Blutner (1998) it is pointed out that the effect of the Gricean maxims is simply to constrain the relation defined by GEN in a particular way. In this vein, the Q- and the I-principle can be seen as conditions constraining possible enrichment pairs $<f, m>$. The precise formulation assumes the availability of the (partial) ordering $\prec$ and formulates a two-way optimization procedure:

(16) a. $<f, m>$ satisfies the Q-principle iff $<f, m> \in GEN$ and there is no distinct pair $<f', m>$ such that $<f', m> \prec <f, m>$.

    b. $<f, m>$ satisfies the I-principle iff $<f, m> \in GEN$ and there is no distinct pair $<f, m'>$ such that $<f, m'> \prec <f, m>$.[8]

---

[6] Roughly, this cost is correlated with the surprise that the particular enrichment m has for an agent confronted with the underlying form f.

[7] Obviously, the cost function can be used to define the ordering, but not vice versa. The connection is as follows: $<f', m> \prec <f, m>$ iff $\underline{c}(f', m) < \underline{c}(f, m)$.

[8] Being more precize, we should write $\prec_\sigma$ and GEN_σ in order to indicate the dependence on the actual context σ. We can drop the index because here and in the following we assume the actual context to be fixed.

In this (rather symmetrical) formulation, the Q- and the I-principle constrain the possible enrichment pairs in two different ways. The I-principle constrains them by selecting the most economic/harmonic enrichments, and the Q-principle constrains them by blocking those enrichments which can be grasped more economically/harmonically by an alternative linguistic input f'. Obviously, it is the Q-principle that carries the main burden in explaining the blocking effects discussed in Section 4.4.

It is straightforward now to introduce the idea of strong bidirection as a direct combination of the Q- and I-principle; the symbols F and M stand now for an abstract distinction between the two relative levels of form (F) and content (M).

(17) **Bidirectional OT (strong version)**

A form-meaning pair $<F, M>$ is called (bidirectionally) **optimal** if and only if:
Q. there is no distinct pair $<F', M>$ realized by GEN such that $<F', M> \prec <F, M>$.
I. there is no distinct pair $<F, M'>$ realized by GEN such that $<F, M'> \prec <F, M>$.

The formulation of the Q- and I-principle in (16) makes it quite clear that the Gricean maxims can be conceived of in a bidirectional optimality framework which integrates expressive and interpretive optimality.[9] In this vein, the present formalization stresses the point that the Q- and the I-principle have to be seen as different ways of optimization, where the content of optimization is intrinsic to the ordering relation $\prec$.

The distinction between explicature and implicature is of particular importance if it comes to instantiate the general scheme (17). For example, in the case of explicature, we have to specify the pair $<F, M>$ with regard to the form meaning distinction provided by the system of grammar.

On the other hand, we have to replace the abstract form-meaning pairs $<F, M>$ in the scheme (17) by possible enrichment pairs $<f, m>$ if we are looking for a proper formalization of the notion of implicature and pragmatic anomaly. Making use of an auxiliary conception called pragmatic licensing the official definitions are as follows:

---

[9] In fact the ideas of Horn, Atlas, and Levinson were the original inspiration for developing Blutner's (2000) version of bidirectional OT.

(18) a. A possible enrichment pair $<f, m>$ is called **pragmatically licensed** (in a common ground σ) if and only if $<f, m>$ is optimal (i.e., it satisfies the Q- and the I-principle) and m is consistent with σ.

   b. An utterance that corresponds to the (underspecified) semantic representation f is called **pragmatically anomalous** (in σ) if and only if there is no pragmatically licensed possible enrichment pair $<f, m>$.

   c. A proposition p is called a **conversational implicature** of f (in σ) if and only if p is a classical consequence of $\sigma \cup m$ for each m of a pragmatically licensed possible enrichment pair $<f, m>$.

It is not difficult to see how the general mechanism of conversational implicature introduced in (18) reflects four basic features/phenomena that are commonly discussed in connection with conversational implicature and pragmatic anomaly (e.g. Blutner, 1998):

(i)   the non-compositional aspect of conversational implicature;
(ii)   the non-monotonicity of conversational implicature;
(iii) the phenomena of blocking (and deblocking);
(iv)   the general fact that pragmatic anomalies usually do not persist.

First, let us consider compositionality. Almost everything in the formulation of conversational implicature has a non-compositional character: the formulation of both the Q-principle and the I-principle is holistic in addressing a wide range of alternative expressions; the conceptions of informativeness, surprise (measured in terms of conditional probability), and linguistic complexity are non-combinatorial and cannot be reduced to the corresponding properties of the parts of an expression.

Next, our system deals with non-monotonicity. The reason is that the notion of conversational implicature is based on preferred interpretations (via the optimization of possible enrichment pairs). It is the old insight of McCarthy (1980), Shoham (1988), and others that the idea of preferred interpretations establishes a non-monotonic (cumulative) inferential relation.

Third, our system deals with blocking and deblocking. The crucial mechanism involved is due to the Q-principle. In the same way, the present system captures the holistic (field-) effects, which are very important if the extensions of lexical concepts are considered.

The fourth and last point concerns the persistence of anomalies. The general definition of pragmatic anomaly does not simply define this notion as some kind of inconsistency. Instead, non-representational parameters (such as surprise, cue validity, relevance, frequency of use, etc.) are cru-cially involved in controlling the selection and suppression of possible en-richments. Within this setting, typically some kind of garden path effect may arise, which are crucially involved in constituting pragmatic anomaly. Gar-den paths can sometimes be avoided under strengthened contexts. Hence, pragmatic anomalies do not necessarily persist under strengthened contexts. A case in point is the following example, which sounds rather anomalous if uttered out of the blue.

(19) ? The tractors are pumped up.

However, this utterance becomes much better in the context of a garage where cars with flat wheels are contrasted with tractors that have enough air pressure in the wheels.

We will now give a very schematic example in order to illustrate some characteristics of bidirectional OT (see also Chapter 3). Assume that we have two forms f_1 and f_2 which are semantically equivalent. This means that GEN associates the same (mental) models with them, say m_1 and m_2. We stipulate that the form f_1 is less complex (marked) than the form f_1 and that the interpretation m_1 is less complex (marked) than the interpretation m_1.

(20) a. $<f_1, m_1> \prec <f_2, m_1>$
     b. $<f_1, m_2> \prec <f_2, m_2>$
     c. $<f_1, m_1> \prec <f_1, m_2>$
     d. $<f_2, m_1> \prec <f_2, m_2>$

From these differences of markedness with regard to the levels of syntactic forms/semantic interpretations, the following ordering relation between form-meaning pairs can be derived:

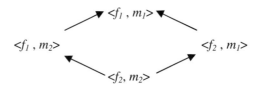

Figure 3   Ordering relation between form-meaning pairs

The results of a bidirectional OT analysis can be represented in **arrow dia-grams**, due to Dekker and van Rooy (2000), who note parallels between the bidirectional OT and basic solution concepts in Game Theory.[10] Here, the arrows represent the preferences between the pairs (the arrows point to the preferred pairs). Arrow diagrams give an intuitive visualization for the optimal pairs of (strong) bidirectional OT: they are simply the hollows if we follow the arcs. The optimal pairs are marked with the symbol ✌ in the diagram.

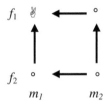

Figure 4   An arrow diagram illustrating total blocking

The scenario just installed describes the case of **total blocking** where some forms (e.g. *furiosity, *fallacity) do not exist because others do *(fury, fallacy)*. However, as noted in Section 4.4, blocking is not always total but may be **partial**, in that only those interpretations of a form are ruled out that are pre-empted by a 'cheaper' competing form.

Cases of total and partial blocking are not only found in morphology, but in syntax and semantics as well (cf. Atlas & Levinson, 1981; Horn, 1984; Williams, 1997). The general tendency of partial blocking seems to be that 'unmarked forms tend to be used for unmarked situations and marked forms for marked situations' (Horn 1984: 26), a tendency that Horn terms the **division of pragmatic labor** (see Chapter 3).

We have seen that the strong form of bidirectionality describes total blocking and does not account for partial blocking. There are two principal possibilities for avoiding the fatal consequences of total blocking. The first possibility is to make some stipulations concerning GEN in order to exclude equivalent semantic forms. The second possibility is to weaken the notion of (strong) optimality in a way that allows us to derive Horn's division of pragmatic labor in a principled way by means of a sophisticated optimization procedure.

---

[10] In short, Dekker and van Rooy (2000) give bidirectional OT a game theoretic interpretation where the optimal pairs can be characterized as so-called Nash equilibria.

In Blutner (1998, 2000) it is argued that the second option is much more practicable and theoretically interesting. It is not difficult to see that the phenomenon of partial blocking clearly calls for a version of bidirectional OT where the two directions of optimization refer to one another. Such a formalization has been given in Blutner (2000). The **weak bidirectional optimality** or super-optimality inexorably links the Q- and I-criteria above so that the evaluations that determine optimality for the two perspectives (expressive versus interpretive) are no longer completely independent of each other, but entirely interdependent.

(21) **Bidirectional OT (weak version)**

A form-meaning pair $<F, M>$ is called **super-optimal** if and only if:
Q. there is no distinct pair $<F', M>$ such that $<F', M> \prec <F, M>$ and $<F', M>$ satisfies I.
I. there is no distinct pair $<F, M'>$ such that $<F, M'> \prec <F, M>$ and $<F, M'>$ satisfies Q.

Following the exposition of weak bidirection in Mattausch (2004a), the point of the definition above is that for a pair $<F, M>$ to fail to be super-optimal, it is not enough that there be a distinct pair $<F', M>$ or $<F, M'>$ that outperforms $<F, M>$. Rather, $<F, M>$ lacks super-optimal status only if there is a superior pair $<F', M>$ or $<F, M'>$ and the superior pair is itself super-optimal.

At first glance, such a definition might seem a bit bewildering, for the definition for satisfaction of the Q-condition is included in the definition for satisfaction of I-condition, which is in turn is included in the definition for satisfaction of the Q-condition. However, as Jäger, who has explored the formal properties of superoptimal evaluation, points out (Jäger, 2002), the definition is not circular as long as we assume that the $\prec$ relation is a well-founded one. Further, Jäger showed the equivalence of (21) with the following recursive formulation (22):

(22) **Bidirectional OT (weak version in Jäger's formulation)**

A form-meaning pair $<F, M>$ is called super-optimal if and only if:
Q. there is no distinct super-optimal pair $<F', M>$ such that $<F', M> \prec <F, M>$.
I. there is no distinct super-optimal pair $<F, M'>$ such that $<F, M'> \prec <F, M>$.

In addition, he proved that each pair which is optimal (strong bidirection) is super-optimal (weak bidirection) as well, but not vice versa. Hence, weak bidirection gives us a chance to find additional, super-optimal solutions. For example, weak bidirection allows marked expressions to have an optimal interpretation, although both the expression and the situations they describe have a more efficient counterpart.

To make this point clear, consider again the situation illustrated in (20) referring to the mental models m and m' and the forms f and f'. Let us apply now the weak version of bidirectional optimization as demonstrated in the arrow diagram in Figure 5. In order to make things more concrete we can take f_1 to be the lexical causative form (12a), f_2 the periphrastic form (12b), m_1 direct (stereotypic) causation and m_2 indirect causation.

(12) a. Black Bart killed the sheriff.
b. Black Bart caused the sheriff to die.

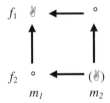

Figure 5 An arrow diagram illustrating partial blocking

While the arrow diagram in Figure 5 involves only one strongly bidirectionally optimal pair, both the pair $<f_1, m_1>$ and $<f_2, m_2>$ are super-optimal.[11] Specifically, though the pair $<f_2, m_2>$ is not strongly bidirectionally optimal, that pair is indeed super-optimal, exactly because there is no super-optimal pair that blocks it (indeed, the two candidates $<f_1, m_2>$ and $<f_2, m_1>$ are not super-optimal, simply because they are blocked by $<f_1, m_1>$)

We have seen that the strong version cannot explain why the marked form f_2 has an interpretation. The weak version, however, can explain this fact. Moreover, it explains that the marked form f_2 gets the atypical interpretation m_2. Recall that we used this explanatory tool to account for the

---

[11] In the diagram, strongly optimal possible enrichment pairs are marked ✌; super-optimal pairs are that are not strongly optimal are marked by (✌).

Dutch scrambling data in Chapter 3. In this way, the weak version of bidirection accounts in a principled way for Horn's division of pragmatic labor. Jäger (2002) has shown that this pattern can be generalized to systems where more than two forms are associated by GEN with more than two interpretations. In the general case, we start with determining the optimal pairs. Then we drop the rows and columns corresponding to the optimal pairs and apply the same procedure to the reduced tableau.[12]

The existence of two notions of bidirectionality raises a conceptual problem: Which conception of bidirectionality is valid, the strong or the weak one? Obviously, this question relates to the foundation of bidirection in an overall framework of cognitive theory. As we will see in the next chapter, the strong mode of optimization in (17) corresponds to an equilibrium established by the OT learning algorithm. When hearer-optimal pairs do not satisfy the principle of strong bidirection then these pairs indicate instabilities of the current OT system (and they trigger changes of the system via the OT learning mechanism).

Weak bidirection gives a chance to find additional solutions. Is it possible to give a natural interpretation for these additional solutions? Elsewhere the idea was proposed that these additional solutions are due to the ability and flexibility of self-organization in language change which the weak formulation alluded to (Blutner & Zeevat, 2004). We come back to this point in Chapter 5.

4.6 An Example: Negative Strengthening

In Section 4.3 a concise description of the phenomenon of negative strengthening was given. Now we will bring this phenomenon into play in order to illustrate the general mechanism of pragmatic strengthening, which is formulated by using the method of bidirectional optimization.

In the analysis of Horn (1989) and Levinson (2000) there are some types of negative strengthening that are obviously attributable to the I/R-principle. A clear case is the negation of positive adjectives, which was described in connection with example (9). Here the I/R-principle leads to a pragmatic strengthening effect excluding the middle ground and implying the contrary.

---

[12] The recursive notation of bidirection accounts for the interaction between Q and I/R that is informally expressed already in Horn (1984). The advantage of the present formalization is that it allows us to prove the general pattern of iconicity (subsuming Horn's division of pragmatic labour; Wurzel's (1998) constructional iconicity and Levinson's (2000) M-principle, the latter expressing the second half of the pattern only.)

The situation is not so clear in the case of adjectives with incorporated affixal negation such as in example (10). Whereas Horn (1984, 1989) seems to attribute the observed effect of negative strengthening to the interaction between Q and R, Levinson stipulates a third pragmatic principle, the M(anner)-principle: 'what's said in a abnormal way, isn't normal; or marked message indicates marked situation.' (Levinson, 2000: 33). Obviously, this principle expresses the second half of Horn's division of pragmatic labor or the markedness principle as it was introduced in Chapter 3.[13]

Let us see now how bidirectional OT accounts for the effects of negative strengthening. Bidirectional Figure 6 shows the competing candidate forms in the left column. Take the candidate entries as shortcuts for complete sentences; for example take *happy* as abbreviating *I'm happy*, etc. The other columns are for the three possible states of happiness considered in this simplified analysis. The grey areas in the figure indicate which form-model pairs are excluded by the compositional mode of truth-functional semantics. For example, *I'm not unhappy* is assumed to exclude the state iconized by ☹.

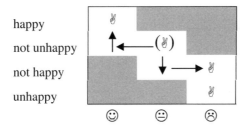

Figure 6   A bidirectional OT analysis of negative strengthening

---

[13] In our opinion, Levinson (2000) tries to turn a plausible heuristic classification scheme based on the three principles Q, I, and M into a general theory by stipulating a ranking Q > M > I. Accepting the heuristic classification schema, we see problems for this theory, which is burdened with too many stipulations. Not unlike Horn's conception, we prefer to see the M-principle as an epiphenomenon that results from the interaction of Zipf's (1949) two 'economy principles' (Q and R in Horn's terminology).

The preferences between the form-model pairs are due to markedness constraints for forms and markedness constraints for interpretations, respectively.

With regard to the forms, we simply assume that the number of negation morphemes is the crucial indicator. The corresponding preferences are indicated by the vertical arrows. Note that *not happy* and *unhappy* are not differentiated in terms of markedness, a rough simplification, of course.

With regard to the states, we assume that they are decreasing in markedness towards both ends of the scale, assigning maximal markedness to the middle ground. Although this assumption seems not implausible from a psycholinguistic perspective, we cannot provide independent evidence for it at the moment. In Figure 6, the corresponding preferences are indicated by the horizontal arrows.

Now it is a simple exercise to find out the optimal solutions, indicated by ☝. One optimal solution pairs the sentence *I'm not happy* with the state indicated by ☹. This solution corresponds to the effect of negative strengthening that is attributable to the I/R-principle. The other two optimal solutions are reflecting the truth condition of *I'm happy/unhappy*.

Most interesting, there is an additional super-optimal solution, indicated by (☝). It pairs the sentence *I'm not unhappy* with the state ☺. This corresponds to the effect of negative strengthening in the case of litotes, normally attributed to Levinson's (2000) M-principle or Horn's division of pragmatic labor. As already stressed, this solution comes out as a natural consequence of the weak form of bidirection, which can be seen as a formal way of describing the interactions between Q and I/R.

It is an interesting exercise to introduce more than three states of happiness and to verify that the proper shape of implicature as indicated in Figure 1 and 2 can be approximated. More importantly, in the context of litotes it seems necessary to account for the effect of gradient acceptability and continuous scales. Using a stochastic evaluation procedure, Boersma (1998) and Boersma and Hayes (2001) did pioneering work in this field, which should be exploited in the present case (see Chapter 5 for a concise discussion of this work).

4.7 Summary

In this chapter we made use of the distinction between explicature and implicature (borrowed from relevance theory). Explicature relates to an interpretive mechanism that includes parts of contextual information in order to determine the truth-conditional content of an utterance. Implicature relates to an interpretive mechanism that goes beyond the truth-conditional content. It conforms to conceptual enrichment and reconstruction, and we considered it as the construction of mental models. In our view, both explicatures and implicatures can be formulated within a bidirectional OT framework. Historically, the neo-Gricean explanation of conversational implicatures (Atlas & Levinson, 1981; Horn, 1984) was a main inspiration for bidirectional OT. After discussing some peculiarities of conversational implicatures (non-monotonicity, blocking), a concise formulation of basic concepts of pragmatics was given in Section 4.5. These ideas were illustrated in the last section by analyzing the phenomenon of negative strengthening in bidirectional OT.

5

Learning

5.1 Introduction

In this chapter we discuss the strong connection between bidirectionality and OT learning theories, and also discuss child language acquisition. It is demonstrated that OT learning theories are intimately connected with the trait of bidirectionality. In addition, we will solve the conceptual problem that is raised by the existence of *two* notions of bidirectionality: the strong and the weak one. Which conception of bidirectionality is valid then? We will argue that children's early forms and meanings are consistent with strong bidirectionality. Only later, from the age of 6 or 7 on, are their forms and meanings consistent with weak bidirectionality. This suggests that both notions of bidirectionality are required for describing and explaining the entire spectrum of forms and meanings in natural language. Alternatively, we will develop an argument that relates the two notions of bidirectionality to different forms of learning. In this connection, we have to accept a very broad view of learning, a view that also includes the evolutionary aspects of learning within a population of language users.

5.2 Constraint Demotion

OT defines a grammar as a ranked set of violable constraints. A general assumption within standard OT is that the constraints are all universal and that only their ranking is language-specific. This assumption betrays the generative tradition in which many representatives of OT were brought up. To a certain extent, this distinction in OT between universal constraints and language-specific rankings reflects the distinction in Principles and Parameters (PP) models between universal principles and language-specific parameter settings. But whereas in PP models the parameters of an innate Universal Grammar (UG) are assumed to be fixed by the presence of certain triggers in the learning data (cf. Gibson & Wexler, 1994), OT takes a different perspective on language learning. In this section, we will discuss Tesar and Smolensky's (2000) **Error-Driven Constraint Demotion Algorithm** for language acquisition.

As in PP models, universal aspects of OT such as the constraints themselves are assumed to be innate. Therefore, the task for a child of learning the grammar of her language consists of learning the particular constraint ranking of her language. This is not an easy task, because the child only receives positive evidence about the grammar that she is learning. This means that she only receives information about which sentences belong to the grammar. This positive evidence is presented to the child in the form of the overt sentences that she encounters. The child does not receive any negative evidence, that is, information about sentences not belonging to the grammar. This absence of negative evidence in the learning data has led many linguists to believe that the learning data is in fact too impoverished to allow successful learning of the grammar just from scratch. This is called the logical problem of language acquisition. Because the learning data is so impoverished, it is commonly assumed that the space of possible grammars should be highly restricted, for example by only allowing for a finite number of parameters distinguishing languages from one another.

But let us look at the overt learning data available to a child from an OT perspective. What information about the correct ranking of the constraints can the child extract from these overt sentences? In OT, overt sentences are the outputs corresponding to certain inputs. Since outputs in OT are only optimal in comparison with competing candidates, the role of competing candidates must be considered too. From the fact that a particular output is grammatical it can be concluded that this output must be less offending than all competing candidates. Each grammatical output, thus, brings with it a body of implicit negative evidence in the form of these suboptimal competitors. This is the basic idea behind Tesar and Smolensky's (2000) OT learning mechanism.

To demonstrate the workings of their learning mechanism, let us look at a concrete example, namely the distribution of subjects (e.g. Grimshaw & Samek-Lodovici, 1998). Although it is generally true that sentences have a subject, in certain languages sentences may appear without a subject. For example, in Italian, pronominal subjects may be dropped if they refer to the discourse topic. Grimshaw and Samek-Lodovici explain these facts through the following constraints (adapted slightly; a fifth constraint for aligning focused constituents is omitted):

(1) SUBJECT: A clause must have a subject in canonical position.
(2) FULL-INT: Constituents in the output must be interpreted.
(3) DROP-TOPIC: An argument that is coreferential with the topic must be deleted.
(4) PARSE: Input constituents must have a correspondent in the output.

These constraints are potentially in conflict. The constraint DROP-TOPIC requires arguments whose antecedent is a topic to be unexpressed. This constraint thus licenses deletion of a topic-referring subject. SUBJECT and PARSE favor those competitors which express the subject overtly. The ranking of these constraints might be as in (5):

(5) FULL-INT » DROP-TOPIC » PARSE » SUBJECT

Now suppose we wish to express the fact that some male individual who is the current discourse topic sang at some moment in the past. The input is {sing(x), x = topic, x = he, tense = present perfect}. The following candidate outputs are among the candidates generated for this input:

(6) a. [IP he has [sung]]
b. [IP he$_i$ has [t$_i$ sung]]
c. [IP has [t$_i$ sung] he$_i$]]
d. [IP it has [[t$_i$ sung] he$_i$]]

Output (6a) is a clause with no subject. In output (6b), the subject has moved out of the VP into the specifier position of IP. In output (6c), the subject is right-adjoined to VP. Output (6d) is the same as (6c), but with an expletive subject in SpecIP. As Tableau 1 shows, the constraint ranking in (5) favors suppression of topic-referring subjects.

TABLEAU 1
Distribution of subjects

	FULL-INT	DROP-TOPIC	PARSE	SUBJECT
☞ [IP he has [sung]]			*	*
[IP he$_i$ has [t$_i$ sung]]		*!		
[IP has [t$_i$ sung] he$_i$]]		*!		*
[IP it has [[t$_i$ sung] he$_i$]]	*!	*		

If a child wishing to learn English assumes this constraint ranking, she will incorrectly drop topic-referring subjects. To obtain the correct grammar for English, she should rerank these constraints. In particular, PARSE should outrank DROP-TOPIC. Given this adjusted ranking, (6b) would be the optimal candidate, as is the case in English.

Now how does the child in the above mentioned situation decide that she should rerank the constraints? She does this on the basis of an observed mismatch between the optimal output provided by the hypothesized constraint ranking (in the above case, (6a)), and a sentence she encounters (for example, (6b)). Hence, the proposed learning algorithm is **error-driven**. Tesar and Smolensky assume that the child has full access to GEN, and therefore to the competing candidates as well. If the child encounters the English sentence *he has sung*, she should conclude that candidate (6b) is actually less offending than competing candidates, including the hypothesized optimal candidate (6a). This means that the hypothesized constraint ranking is incorrect. Because constraints are ordered according to strict dominance, each winner-loser pair (i.e. each pair consisting of a grammatical output and an ungrammatical competitor) provides the child with essential information about the ranking of the constraints. In particular, it tells the child that the constraints that are violated by the winner must be ranked lower than at least one constraint that is violated by the loser. The constraint ranking can now be adjusted accordingly. Constraints that are violated by the winner must be **demoted** below constraints that are violated by the loser. Note that the inverse of constraint demotion, constraint promotion, would not work. If more than one constraint is violated by the loser, it is not clear which of these constraints should be promoted. This problem does not arise with constraint demotion. Constraints are only demoted as far as necessary. This process of constraint demotion is applied iteratively until the constraints are ranked in such a way that they account for all of the data the child encounters.

Let us return to our example to illustrate this procedure of constraint demotion. According to the grammar entertained by our child who is trying to learn English, the optimal candidate is (6a). However, according to the grammar of English, the optimal candidate is (6b). This is marked by the sign ✓ in the tableau below.

TABLEAU 2
Learning the distribution of subjects

	FULL-INT	DROP-TOPIC	PARSE	SUBJECT
☞ [IP he has [sung]]			*	*
✓ [IP heᵢ has [tᵢ sung]]		*!		

Because the child hears (6b), (6b) is the winner. Therefore, the constraints that are violated by (6b) should be demoted below at least one constraint that is violated by (6a). This means that DROP-TOPIC should be demoted below PARSE. This results in the ranking in (7):

(7) FULL-INT » PARSE » DROP-TOPIC » SUBJECT

If the child adopts this ranking, the Italian-like candidate *has sung* becomes suboptimal and (6b) is correctly selected as the optimal candidate. Note that the ranking in (7) is not yet the correct ranking for English. To arrive at the correct ranking, the child must encounter sentences with expletives, such as *it seems that he has sung*. The presence of the expletive *it*, which violates FULL-INT, will force iterative demotion of this constraint until it is ranked below SUBJECT (see Grimshaw & Samek-Lodovici, 1998).

For the 'correctness' of (iterative) constraint demotion it is important that the OT grammar of the language that has to be learned is based on a total ranking of all the constraints. Tesar and Smolensky (2000) show that the iterative procedure of constraint demotion converges to a set of totally ranked constraint hierarchies, each of them accounting for the learning data. Interestingly, this result holds when starting with an arbitrary constraint hierarchy.

Another important result of Tesar and Smolensky's Error-Driven Constraint Demotion algorithm is that only a relatively small number of informative examples is required to fix the ranking of the constraints and select the correct grammar. If the grammar has n constraints, the number of possible rankings of these constraints is n! (i.e., $n(n-1)(n-2)(n-3)...1$) but the number of informative examples required to learn this grammar is at most $n(n-1)$. In contrast, in a parameterized Universal Grammar with n binary interacting parameters, the average number of triggers required before reaching the target grammar is 2^n. If the parameters are completely independent and non-interacting, PP models fare better, only requiring n^2 triggers. This is comparable to the complexity in OT but, as Tesar and Smolensky conclude, assuming independent parameters with restricted effects for the sake of learnability results in a conflict with the goal of linguistic theory to favor parameters with wide-ranging effects and greater explanatory power.

5.3 The Bootstrap Idea for Learning Hidden Structure

Constraint demotion only gives us half of the mechanism for learning an OT grammar, though. In the above example we overlooked one essential property of language learning: constraints in OT apply to **structural descriptions**. A child learning a language, however, does not encounter structural descriptions but rather hears unstructured strings of sounds. A central problem in language learning is how to extract the hidden structure from an overt sentence. Tesar and Smolensky formulate this problem as follows:

> The learner cannot deduce the hidden structure in learning data until she has learned the grammar, but she cannot learn the grammar until she has the hidden structure. (Tesar & Smolensky, 2000: 7).

The proposed solution is to apply the process of optimization in the opposite direction. This is called **robust interpretive parsing**. Robust interpretive parsing takes an overt structure and optimizes over all structural descriptions that yield this overt structure (see Figure 1). By using this procedure, the optimal structural description, complete with all hidden structure, can be assigned to an overt sentence. This optimal structural description is determined by the current constraint ranking entertained by the child. Robustness refers to the fact that also sentences that are ungrammatical by the currently entertained grammar are assigned structural descriptions. Via the standard procedure of productive parsing[1], which chooses among candidate structural descriptions with the same input the optimal structural description, the child will be able to tell whether this interpretive parse is grammatical or not by her current grammar. If the results of productive parsing and interpretive

---

[1] In the OT literature the term *parsing* is used for the general issue of assigning structure to input. This use of the term should not be confused with the use of the same term in the common context of language comprehension.

parsing are different, then this information is used to correct the grammar. The child then applies constraint demotion, presuming the interpretive parse as the winner and the productive parse as the loser. The child has succeeded in learning the grammar if interpretive and productive parsing always give the same structural description.

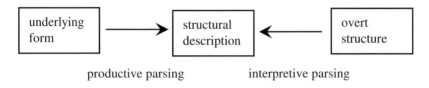

productive parsing   interpretive parsing

Figure 1 Productive and interpretive parsing

The idea of combining robust interpretive parsing and constraint demotion gives a plausible picture of children's acquisition of an OT grammar. The described bootstrap mechanism of a gradual improvement of the children's OT grammar also explains the kind of asymmetry that is found in language acquisition. It is well known that children's ability in production lags behind their ability in comprehension. This asymmetry can be explained by making the assumption that the initial state of OT grammar satisfies the condition that the markedness constraints outrank the faithfulness constraints (Smolensky, 1996).

Learning makes essentially use of the basic assumptions of OT: (i) constraints strictly dominate one another; (ii) the OT grammar that has to be learned is based on a total rather than a partial ranking of the constraints. In applying these basic principles, the learning mechanism exploits the structure of OT. However, it remains an open question whether the assumptions (i) and (ii) are mere oversimplifications made for didactic and practical reasons, or whether they reflect the true nature of OT (see Section 5.4). In a similar vein, it remains to be seen whether all OT constraints are really innate or whether the existence of at least some of the constraints can be explained from a functional perspective (cf. Boersma, 1998).

In Section 5.2 we outlined that the simple mechanism of (iterative) constraint demotion always converges to the target grammar if it is assumed that the target grammar is based on a total ranking of all the constraints. In the case of learning hidden structure where the bootstrap idea is applied for extracting underlying structure from the overt parts of (grammatical) forms, the situation is different and the algorithm sometimes does not converge. Moreover, while the pure constraint demotion algorithm converges independently of the initial constraint hierarchy, the convergence of the combined algorithm is highly sensitive to the initial hierarchy. Tesar and Smolensky (2000) have demonstrated this fact by simulation experiments investigating the task of learning metrical stress grammar (based on a system of 12 constraints). Using a sample of 124 languages and a set of 62 overt forms for each of them, the results suggest that the full algorithm is practicable in case the initial hierarchy is appropriate. A general condition seems to be that faithfulness constraints are dominated by the structural constraints. This assumption corresponds to a general hypothesis in children's acquisition of phonology, and it is used, for example, to explain that children's ability in production lags behind their ability in comprehension. Although there is much to do in order to find out the effect of specific starting hierarchies, the simulation experiments demonstrate convincingly that in the relevant cases the speed of convergence is surprisingly high and qualitatively different from that of general search procedures over parametric spaces (such as the triggering learning algorithm in the PP model).

For the following it is important to make a distinction between autoassociative learning (with its ability to extract structure from a given overt input pattern) and pattern association (learning the relation between two relatively independent sets of stimuli). Whereas the first type of learning in most cases conforms to **unsupervised learning**, the second type of learning normally is **supervised learning**. It is a characteristic of the latter that a second agent ('teacher') is available who controls the first agent and confronts/corrects her with the appropriate pairs of pattern.

We have seen that the bootstrap idea of combining robust interpretive parsing with constraint demotion (Tesar & Smolensky, 2000) conforms to the first kind of learning: extracting structure from a series of overt inputs. We have seen further that this idea leads to successful learning of the grammar if the child's grammar converges to the target grammar: interpretive and productive parsing always give the same structural description under the constraint ranking of the target grammar (see Figure 1). Given that the structural description uniquely determines the overt form and the underlying form (by means of GEN), if the learning algorithm has converged (i.e., under a particular ranking of the constraints) the relation between underlying and overt forms can be described to be symmetric in the following sense: if an overt form produces a certain underlying form, then the underlying form (re)produces the initial overt form. This is similar to the following symmetric relation between forms and meanings: if a form-meaning pair is hearer-optimal, then it also is speaker-optimal (and thus satisfies strong bidirectionality). In other words, if a hearer-optimal form-meaning pair does not satisfy the principle of strong bidirectionality then this pair indicates instability of the current OT system. Such a pair is crucial as a trigger of the OT learning mechanism. We can conclude that strong bidirectionality relates to a synchronic law that describes the equilibrium that results from successful learning.

5.4 Pattern Association and Bidirectional Learning

It is generally assumed that for natural languages the form-meaning relation is arbitrary to some extent. Consequently, it needs a mechanism of supervised learning in order to find the correct pairing between form-meaning pairs. Crucially, finding structure in overt inputs is important both for analyzing natural language forms and natural language meanings. However, it is not enough. It is also important to learn the relation between the two levels of representation. Hence, we are confronted with the problem of pattern association.

Let us consider a simple experimental situation where a subject is presented with a (repeated) series of pairs of pattern. The subject has to learn that when one member of the pair is presented it is supposed to produce the other. Hence, in this paradigm the subject has to learn a predefined relation between a set of input patterns with a set of output patterns. For example, an input pattern can be a lexigram (e.g. senseless syllable), and an output pattern can be a picture of a fruit. We assume a 1-1 correspondence between syllables and pictures.

If subjects are qualified to match Stimulus A to B and then, without further training, match B to A, they have passed a **test of symmetry**. The important empirical finding is that children as young as 2 years pass the symmetry test (e.g. Green, 1990). In contrast, chimps did not show symmetry: having learned to match lexigram comparisons to object samples, the chimps were not able, without further training, to match the same objects now presented as comparisons to the corresponding lexigrams, now presented as samples (Dugdale & Lowe, 2000; Savage-Rumbaugh, 1984).[2]

Assuming that OT is appropriate to describe the knowledge underlying subject's pattern association in concrete experimental situations, we can take the test of symmetry as relating to strong bidirection. If A => B ('hearer' perspective) then B => A ('speaker' perspective), and vice versa. As a consequence, all hearer-optimal pairs are strongly optimal if they pass the test of symmetry; the same holds for speaker-optimal pairs.

---

[2] A possible exception is Kanzi, the bonobo monkey. Kanzi's knowledge was reciprocal. There was no need to teach her separately to produce and to comprehend (Savage-Rumbaugh & Lewin, 1994).

Symmetry seems to build in the basic learning mechanism of human beings (but not of chimps). In order to model this important feature of human learning within the framework of OT, we simply have to apply constraint demotion twice. Where our learner is faced with a learning datum A-B, she not only has to learn to join B given A but also to join A given B. In this way, some constraints may be affected only by hearer learning modes, some other constraints only by speaker learning modes, and a third group of constraints by both hearer- and speaker- learning modes. Section 5.7 outlines a concrete realization of this idea of bidirectional learning, Jäger's gradual learning algorithm (cf. Jäger, 2004). At this occasion, the idea of bidirectional learning is realized within Boersma's framework of gradual learning (Boersma, 1998; Boersma & Hayes, 2001).

In the next section we take an empirical perspective on bidirectional learning and report some recent results concerning child language acquisition of the form-meaning relationship for indefinite subjects and objects.

5.5 Acquisition of Indefinite Subject and Object Interpretation in Dutch

De Hoop and Krämer (2004) find a general, language-independent pattern in child language acquisition in which there is a clear difference between subject and object noun phrases. They explain this pattern within the framework of bidirectional OT. They focus on clarifying the nature of the linguistic knowledge that a 4-year old child will need to acquire in order to become a competent, adult like user of her language. In this section we will briefly discuss their approach.

Consider the Dutch sentences below:

(8)	Je	mag	twee	keer	een	potje	omdraaien.
	you	may	two	time	a	pot	around-turn

'You may turn a pot twice.'

(9)	Je	mag	een	potje	twee	keer	omdraaien.
	you	may	a	pot	two	time	around-turn

'You may turn a pot twice.'

Recall from Chapter 3 that in Dutch, the indefinite object noun phrase can either occur to the right of the adverbial phrase *twee keer* 'twice' as in (8), or it can occur to the left of it, as in (9). The left position in (9) is referred to as the scrambled position, the right position in (8) as the unscrambled position. Krämer (2000) tested the interpretation of scrambled and unscrambled indefinite objects in children between 4;0 and 8;0. Children as well as adults get a non-referential reading for the unscrambled indefinite. That is, when asked to act out (8) both children and adults turn two pots. For most children below age 7, however, the scrambled indefinites are also interpreted non-referentially, whereas adults always interpret the scrambled indefinites referentially. So, while adults respond to (9) by turning one pot twice, children turn two pots, just as they did in response to (8).

The Dutch data seem to be in accordance with cross-linguistic data showing that children between roughly 4 and 6 years old prefer to interpret the object noun phrases non-referentially, even in situations when adults interpret them referentially (cf. de Hoop and Krämer, 2004, for references).

On the other hand, for the interpretation of indefinite *subjects*, the picture is completely different. In a number of experiments, children, just like adults, provided nearly exclusively referential interpretations of indefinite subject noun phrases. With regard to Dutch, Bergsma-Klein (1996) found that children correctly assign a referential ('wide scope') reading to indefinite subjects as in (10).

(10) Een   meisje   gleed   twee   keer   uit.
     A   girl   slipped two   time   out$_{PARTICLE}$
     'A girl slipped twice.'

De Hoop and Krämer (2004) conclude that cross-linguistically there happens to exist a subject-object asymmetry in children's interpretation of indefinites. When adults assign a referential interpretation to indefinite subjects, children generally do the same. But when adults assign a referential interpretation to indefinite objects, children cross-linguistically do *not* do the same.

The asymmetry can be further extended, as shown by de Hoop and Krämer (2004), when we consider the non-referential interpretation of indefinites. That is, when adults assign a non-referential ('narrow scope') reading to an object, so do children. For example, 100% of the children between 4;0 and 6;10 years old correctly interpret the indefinite object in (11) non-referentially (Krämer, 2000).

(11) Het   meisje   heeft   geen   appel   geplukt.
     The   girl   has   no   apple   picked
     'The girl didn't pick an apple.'

A final piece of evidence for the subject-object asymmetry concerns the non-referential reading of indefinite subjects. Termeer (2002) found that when adults assign a non-referential interpretation to a subject, children prefer a referential interpretation. That is, only 32% of the children between age 8;7 and 10;4 get an adult-like non-referential ('narrow scope') reading for the embedded indefinite subject in (12) (Termeer, 2002).

(12) Er   ging   twee   keer een   jongen   van de   glijbaan   af.
      There went   two   time a   boy   of   the   slide   off
      'Twice, there went a boy down the slide.'

In conclusion, children are adult-like in their interpretation of referential indefinite subjects and in their interpretation of non-referential indefinite objects. They differ from adults when they have to interpret non-referential indefinite subjects and when they have to interpret referential indefinite objects. How can we explain this pattern? Note that cross-linguistically subjects outrank objects in referentiality. It is a well-known typological generalization, supported by statistical evidence, that subjects tend to be referential, definite, topical, animate, high-prominent in the discourse, among other notions, while objects tend to be non-referential, indefinite, inanimate, low-prominent in the discourse (Aissen, 2003; Comrie, 1989; Lee, 2003). Children seem to behave in accordance with that generalization, that is, they assign a referential interpretation to subjects and a non-referential interpretation to objects. Adults, however, can depart from this pattern when required. More precisely, they are able to assign a non-referential reading to indefinite subjects, and a referential reading to indefinite objects. Children's non-adultlike interpretations of the example sentences above can be characterized as a failure to depart from the general pattern. Why do children fail in this respect? De Hoop and Krämer (2004) provide a bidirectional Optimality Theoretic account of this pattern. This account can straightforwardly explain why children deviate from the adult pattern in exactly the way they do.

In Chapter 3, Section 5, we introduced the following constraints for our bidirectional analysis of the scrambling behavior of indefinite objects:

(13) MEANING INDEFINITE OBJECT (MIO): An indefinite object gets a non-referential reading (presumably type $<e,t>$).

(14) FORM INDEFINITE OBJECT (FIO): An indefinite object does not scramble.

For our purposes here, we need two similar constraints for the interpretation of subjects:

(15) MEANING INDEFINITE SUBJECT (MIS): An indefinite subject gets a referential reading (presumably type *e*).

(16) FORM INDEFINITE SUBJECT (FIS): An indefinite subject is in the standard subject position [Spec, IP].

These four constraints will give us the unmarked meanings of indefinite subjects and objects as the optimal candidates from an interpretive point of view, and the unmarked forms from an expressive point of view. These constraints, however, cannot account for the marked meanings (and neither for the marked forms).

However, marked meanings of indefinite subjects and objects do occur. Adult speakers of English can easily interpret an indefinite object both non-referentially (the unmarked reading) and referentially (the marked reading). Similarly, indefinite subjects such receive either an unmarked, referential, or a marked, non-referential, reading in English. Both with respect to indefinite objects as with respect to indefinite subjects, the marked reading can be the optimal reading of the unmarked form within a certain context. In some cases, the unmarked form is the only form available. This holds for instance for the indefinite direct objects in English. But as for the indefinite subjects in English and Dutch and the indefinite objects in Dutch, there is an alternative, 'marked' form available. And when a marked form is used, the marked reading emerges irrespective of the context. That is, adult hearers of Dutch interpret a scrambled indefinite object referentially, even in the absence of any further contextual or prosodic information. As we have seen already in Chapter 3, bidirectional OT (Blutner, 2000) provides us with a straightforward explanation of how these unmarked and marked form-meaning pairs arise.

Let us now give a bidirectional OT analysis of the data under discussion in this section; the first tableau is repeated from Chapter 3, Section 5.

TABLEAU 3
Bidirectional OT analysis of indefinite objects

Input: Indefinite object	FIO	MIO
☞ <[unscrambled], <e,t>>	✓	✓
<[scrambled], <e,t>>	*	✓
<[unscrambled], e>	✓	*
☞ <[scrambled], e>	*	*

In the above tableau we see that although the indefinite object that combines a referential meaning with a scrambled word order violates both constraints, it does represent a super-optimal pair, simply because there is no super-optimal pair available that has either a more harmonic form or a more harmonic meaning. The only other super-optimal pair has both a more harmonic form and a more harmonic meaning and therefore it cannot block the 'marked' super-optimal pair. Thus, the bidirectional OT approach straightforwardly accounts for the scrambling phenomenon of indefinite objects in Dutch.

A similar analysis can be provided for the possible forms and meanings of indefinite subjects, as illustrated below.

TABLEAU 4
Bidirectional OT analysis of indefinite subjects

Input: indefinite subjects	FIS	MIS
☞ <[Spec, IP], e>	✓	✓
<[Spec, VP], e>	*	✓
<[Spec, IP], <e,t>>	✓	*
☞ <[Spec, VP], <e,t>>	*	*

One super-optimal pair links the unmarked (referential) meaning to the unmarked position (the standard subject position) while the other super-optimal pair links the marked (non-referential) meaning to the marked position (the embedded subject position).

In conclusion, we find that a bidirectional OT analysis straightforwardly explains the adult pattern of the interpretation of both indefinite objects and indefinite subjects. Adults are able to evaluate form-meaning pairs. That means that they cannot only find the optimal form for a certain meaning or the optimal meaning of a certain form, they are also capable of determining as a super-optimal pair the combination of a form that is sub-optimal from a unidirectional syntactic perspective and a meaning that is sub-optimal from a unidirectional semantic perspective.

We would now like to use the bidirectional OT framework for our explanation of the children's pattern of interpreting indefinite subjects and objects. Clearly, as soon as children have acquired the relevant constraints and their ranking, they will assign a non-referential reading to indefinite objects and a referential reading to indefinite subjects, independent of the position these noun phrases occupy.[3] This is exactly in accordance with what has been attested in the experiments, as discussed above. In other words, these results indicate that children have acquired the interpretive constraints and therefore they can determine the optimal meaning of the optimal form (that is, the 'unmarked' super-optimal pair).

But children deviate from adult's interpretations, when they are required to arrive at a 'marked' meaning. Sometimes this is due to the fact that the children do not have acquired all the relevant cross-modular constraints yet or that they have not yet captured the right weighting or ranking of these constraints. They have difficulties in integrating the information from the context and the intonational pattern into their interpretation of the form. A different explanation is available when children do not obtain a marked meaning of a marked form. In that particular case, it seems that they optimize the interpretation of the marked (e.g. scrambled) form unidirectionally instead of bidirectionally. Thus, children's optimal interpretation of a marked form will be the same as their optimal interpretation of an unmarked form in the same context. In that case, we predict a non-referential reading of the indefinite object in scrambled position and a referential reading of the indefinite subject in embedded subject position.

In order to get the right interpretation for the indefinite subject or object in a marked position, however, the child must apply the process of optimization bidirectionally. One hypothesis that explains this mental ability is that the child has acquired some skill of 'mindreading'. What is needed is the following 'reasoning' by the child: I can find the optimal interpretation for this form, but I notice that the form is sub-optimal; the speaker would have used the optimal form for the optimal meaning (the 'unmarked' super-optimal form-meaning pair), therefore I must choose the sub-optimal meaning for this sub-optimal form, which will give me another ('marked') super-optimal form-meaning pair.

We think that this bidirectional OT analysis of indefinite subject and object interpretation clarifies in what sense children's interpretations deviate from the adult interpretations. Obviously, they might also have problems in determining the optimal interpretation in a certain context independently of the markedness of the form. But they definitely fail when they have to assign a sub-optimal (marked) reading to a sub-optimal (marked) form. Before the

---

3 De Hoop and Krämer assume that MIO and MIS are both the outcome of two constraints, one dealing with the canonical interpretation of indefinite noun phrases as non-referential, the other dealing with the canonical interpretation of subjects/objects as referential/non-referential, respectively.

4-year old child will be a competent, adultlike hearer of her language, she must acquire the full process of optimization of interpretation, which crucially also involves taking into account the speaker perspective of optimization in a bidirectional approach.

In Section 5.7 we will argue that the hypothesis of the child's rising ability of 'mind reading' is not the only possibility to make sense of weak bidirectionality. Instead of seeing the process of bidirectional optimization as a pure **on-line** mechanism we also can consider it as an **off-line** mechanism. The nature of this off-line mechanism relates to some memory based process. From a functionalist perspective it can be described as a freezing mechanism (freezing the effects of weak bidirectionality, i.e. freezing the relevant conversational implicatures) or an automatization mechanism (in the sense of an instance theory of automatization; cf. Logan, 1988). What hypothesis is correct – the on-line theory or the off-line theory – is undecided at the moment.

5.6 Children's Optimal Interpretation of Pronouns

In the previous section, we presented an account of children's acquisition of the optimal interpretation of indefinite subjects and objects. In this section, we argue that a similar developmental process occurs in relation to the acquisition of pronominal interpretations. The analysis discussed in this section is based on work presented in Hendriks and Spenader (2004).

One of the core issues in syntactic theory is binding. In its standard formulation (Chomsky, 1981), Binding Theory consists of three principles. The first principle is concerned with the behavior of reflexives, the second one with the behavior of pronouns, and the third one (which we omit because of its irrelevance to the present discussion) with the behavior of referential expressions:

(17) **Binding Theory**

    Principle A: A reflexive must be bound locally.
    Principle B: A pronoun must be free locally.

According to the standard formulation of Binding Theory, Principle A and Principle B entail complementarity between reflexives and pronouns. Although this is true in many contexts, there are a number of contexts where this complementarity breaks down. Here we will be concerned with the basic pattern only, but see Hendriks and Spenader (in preparation) for a discussion of these exceptional cases.

It is often argued that knowledge of the binding principles is innate. Therefore, children are expected to conform to Binding Theory as soon as they understand the basic properties of syntax. However, there appears to be a clear asymmetry in children's pattern of acquisition of the binding principles A and B. Children correctly interpret reflexives like adults from the age of 3;0, but they continue to perform poorly on the interpretation of pronouns even up to the age of 6;6 (Grimshaw & Rosen, 1990; Wexler & Chien, 1985). For example, sentences like (18) are correctly understood from a young age (95% of the time, according to some studies), but the *him* in (19) is misinterpreted as coreferring with the subject about half the time, which seems to be the result of chance performance.

(18) Bert saw himself.

(19) Bert saw him.

For this **Pronoun Interpretation Problem** (sometimes referred to as Delay of Principle B Effect), a good explanation has yet to be given. There are several strategies to deal with these data. Reinhart (1983) and Chien and Wexler (1990) revise Principle B so that (19) is no longer governed by it, making a distinction between syntactic coindexing and pragmatic coreference. As a result, another explanation has to be found for the interpretation of the pronoun in (19). One of the main arguments for this approach is that children seem to correctly interpret pronouns in the scope of quantified noun phrases. This shows knowledge of syntactic coindexing. However, experimental results here are unclear, with some experiments finding children able to interpret these pronouns (Chien & Wexler, 1990), while other experiments have found that children have trouble with these pronouns as well (Jakubowicz, 1991; Koster, 1993). Also, it is theoretically a matter of dispute whether pronouns in the scope of quantified noun phrases pattern with reflexives (Grodzinsky & Reinhart, 1993) or with pronouns as in (19) (Chien & Wexler, 1990) with respect to the analysis they should receive. An alternative strategy to account for the Pronoun Interpretation Problem, followed by Grimshaw and Rosen (1990), is to argue that (19) is governed by Principle B but that children do not always obey this principle in an experimental setting. A problem with such an account is that it is unable to explain why children behave so differently with respect to reflexives and pronouns. Grimshaw and Rosen's solution is to disconnect Principle A from Principle B, arguing that 'Knowledge of Principle A is logically independent of Principle B' (Grimshaw & Rosen, 1990: 197). However, this does not seem to be in accordance with the empirical data. As Burzio (1998) points out, pronouns seem to fill the space from which reflexives are excluded.

Children's production data complicate the picture. Bloom et al. (1994) studied the spontaneous production of the English pronoun *me* and the reflexive *myself* in data from the CHILDES database. By age 2;3 - 3;1 the children that were studied consistently used the pronoun to express a disjoint meaning (99.8% correct), while they used the reflexive to express a coreferential meaning (93.5%). Bloom et al. conclude from these production data that children have competence in binding principles, even if their performance may sometimes indicate otherwise.

In this section, we discuss an explanation proposed by Hendriks and Spenader (2004), who argue that children's lag in pronoun comprehension is due to the late acquisition of the ability to reason bidirectionally. Their explanation handles both examples (18) and (19) and is consistent with the majority of the experimental results of children's production and comprehension of reflexives and pronouns. The explanation suggested by Hendriks and Spenader is based on the analysis of reflexives and pronouns proposed by Burzio (1998) within an OT syntax framework. Burzio argues that it is difficult, if not impossible, to describe the behavior of anaphoric expressions cross-linguistically in terms of their morphological class, because the function of an anaphoric expression is affected by what other referential devices are present in a given language. Therefore, the behavior of anaphoric expressions is most adequately described in terms of implicational hierarchies, which can be straightforwardly translated into soft OT constraints. Burzio (1998) proposes a soft-constraint alternative to the Principles A, B and C of Binding Theory which is based on the following two constraints:

(20) Burzio's (1998) constraints:

PRINCIPLE A: A reflexive must be bound locally.

REFERENTIAL ECONOMY: a » b » c
a. bound NP = reflexive
b. bound NP = pronoun
c. bound NP = R-expression

Although Burzio does not do so himself, we will refer to the first constraint as PRINCIPLE A, since its effects are similar to that of Principle A of Binding Theory. The second constraint, which Burzio terms REFERENTIAL ECONOMY, actually consists of three constraints which are ranked with respect to each other. REFERENTIAL ECONOMY reflects the view that expressions with less referential content are preferred over expressions with more referential content. Because Burzio considers 'reflexives to have no inherent referential content, pronouns to have some, and R-expressions to have full referential content' (Burzio 1998: 93), the effect of this constraint is that reflexives are preferred to pronouns as bound NPs, and pronouns are preferred to R-expressions in these cases.

Burzio proposes these two constraints in order to account for the distribution of reflexives and pronouns. In this section, we are also interested in the interpretation of reflexives and pronouns. Therefore, we have to distinguish the effects of the constraints on the form of an expression from their effects on the interpretation of this expression. The constraint REFERENTIAL ECONOMY can be generalized in such a way that it applies to the form of an expression only. As we will show below, also under this more general formulation an adequate account can be given of the distribution of reflexives and pronouns.

(21) REFERENTIAL ECONOMY: Avoid R-expressions » Avoid pronouns » Avoid reflexives

According to this formulation, certain forms are preferred to other forms, irrespective of their interpretation. Because reflexives are preferred to pronouns, every occurrence of a pronoun yields a more serious violation of REFERENTIAL ECONOMY than any occurrence of a reflexive. If REFERENTIAL ECONOMY were the only constraint applying to the forms in a language, then the only noun phrases occurring in the language would be reflexives. However, the selection of a form is also constrained by PRINCIPLE A. Under Burzio's formulation, which we adopt, PRINCIPLE A establishes a relation between a specific form (a reflexive) and a specific interpretation (a coreferential meaning). Hence, PRINCIPLE A is a constraint on forms as well as meanings. Because PRINCIPLE A is stronger than REFERENTIAL ECONOMY, a reflexive is used only if the speaker intends to express a coreferential meaning. In all other cases, a pronoun or R-expression must be used. Thus, the interaction between these two constraints explains Burzio's observation that pronouns cross-linguistically seem to fill the space from which reflexives are excluded. This observation is extremely difficult to account for in terms of inviolable principles because the exact conditions under which reflexives occur differ cross-linguistically.

The interaction between PRINCIPLE A and REFERENTIAL ECONOMY is able to explain the child language data discussed in the beginning of this section. In production, Tableau 5 predicts that a reflexive is preferred for expressing a coreferential meaning in sentences such as (18) and (19), that is, in sentences where the anaphoric expression and its antecedent occur within the same local domain.

TABLEAU 5
Producing a coreferential meaning

Input: coreferential meaning	PRINCIPLE A	REFERENTIAL ECONOMY
☞ Reflexive form		
pronominal form		*!

For a disjoint meaning, a pronoun is preferred over a reflexive, which violates PRINCIPLE A, as is predicted by Tableau 6.

TABLEAU 6
Producing a disjoint meaning

Input: disjoint meaning	PRINCIPLE A	REFERENTIAL ECONOMY
reflexive form	*!	
☞ pronominal form		*

Tableaux 7 and 8 give the results of interpretation. Because REFERENTIAL ECONOMY is a constraint on forms, it is not relevant here. Thus based on PRINCIPLE A, it is predicted that the optimal interpretation of a reflexive is a coreferential interpretation.

TABLEAU 7
Interpreting a reflexive form

Input: reflexive form	PRINCIPLE A	REFERENTIAL ECONOMY
☞ coreferential meaning		
disjoint meaning	*!	

Because PRINCIPLE A only has an effect when a reflexive is present (i.e., as the input or as a candidate output), it is not relevant when the input form is a pronoun. The result of optimization is thus that both interpretations are equally preferred. This could account for the observation that children perform at chance levels in comprehension experiments.

TABLEAU 8
Interpreting a pronominal form

Input: pronominal form	PRINCIPLE A	REFERENTIAL ECONOMY
☞ coreferential meaning		
☞ disjoint meaning		

So unidirectional optimization from meaning to form explains children's production of reflexives and pronouns. Similarly, unidirectional optimization from form to meaning explains children's interpretation of reflexives and pronouns. But if children begin with unidirectional optimization, what then leads them to acquire the adult-like disjoint interpretation for pronouns at a later stage? Unidirectional learning strategies using constraint reranking will not lead to pronouns being optimally interpreted as disjoint. However, bidirectional optimization, which considers production and comprehension simultaneously, predicts the adult pattern. For our data, given the two meanings and the two forms there are four logically possible form-meaning pairs. The form-meaning pair <reflexive, coreferential> is an optimal pair. It satisfies both constraints under consideration. Bidirectional OT then allows a further round of optimization. The second and third candidate pairs will not be considered in this second round of optimization because they involve a form or a meaning that is part of the already identified optimal pair <reflexive, coreferential>. For this reason, these form-meaning pairs are suboptimal. As a result, the pair <pronoun, disjoint> will be identified as the second super-optimal pair.

TABLEAU 9
A bidirectional analysis of reflexives and pronouns

	PRINCIPLE A	REFERENTIAL ECONOMY
☞ <reflexive, coreferential>	✓	✓
<reflexive, disjoint>	*	✓
<pronoun, coreferential>	✓	*
☞ <pronoun, disjoint>	✓	*

Thus a bidirectional analysis predicts normal adult usage of pronouns and reflexives. This suggests that children begin with unidirectional optimization, and only later acquire the ability to optimize bidirectionally. A child must, when hearing a pronoun, reason about what other non-expressed forms are associated with the potential interpretations of pronouns, realize that a coreferential meaning is better expressed by a reflexive, and then by a process of elimination realize that because this potential meaning is already better expressed by a reflexive, the pronoun should be interpreted as disjoint. Optimizing bidirectionally inherently involves reasoning about alternatives not present in the current situation, which may be a skill acquired very late, thus explaining the lag in acquisition.

This analysis is compatible with ideas in Grodzinsky and Reinhart (1993), who argue that if a coreference interpretation for a pronoun is not distinguishable from a bound variable interpretation (i.e., an interpretation that would be obtained by using a reflexive), the coreference interpretation is blocked. However, rather than postulating a pragmatic rule accounting for the interpretation of pronouns, Hendriks and Spenader derive Principle B effects from Principle A. Note that the treatment of reflexives and pronouns in this differs from the treatment of these elements in Section 1.5 of Chapter 1. In Chapter 1, we simply stipulated Principle B as a constraint on interpretation. In this section it was shown that the effects of this constraint can be derived from Principle A if a bidirectional approach to interpretation is adopted.

Hendriks and Spenader's analysis also parallels the analysis of children's acquisition of the interpretation of indefinites in Dutch put forward in the previous section. It accounts for the Pronoun Interpretation Problem without assuming a more complex version of the binding principles or their parts. Moreover, it does not require that we reject the robust findings of comprehension experiments or the production data obtained by investigating the CHILDES database. Although no disassociation between the system for comprehension and the system for production needs to be posited, the analysis presented here nevertheless predicts that comprehension can lag behind on production. These lags in acquisition are predicted to occur in those cases where comprehension involves reasoning about alternatives. It is this bidirectional optimization, and not the grammatical principles themselves, that seem to be acquired late.

In the previous section we have mentioned another possibility of making sense of weak bidirectionality. Instead of seeing the process of bidirectional optimization as an on-line mechanism we can consider it as an off-line mechanism of freezing the super-optimal solution pairs. In the present context the differences between the two views relate to the status of Principle B. According to the first view the effects of Principle B are on-line derived from Principle A (via some mechanism of 'mind reading' that conforms to the logic of weak bidirectionality).[4] According to the alternative view some off-line mechanism of freezing/automatization takes place that constitutes Principle B as a real constraint on interpretation. In Section 5.8 the on-line and the off-line view are discussed in more detail. A requisite for understanding the off-line view is the theory of bidirectional learning which we will explain in the following section.

5.7 The Gradual Learning Algorithm and Bidirectional Learning

In Section 5.3 we stressed a fundamental assumption of Tesar and Smolensky's learning theory: The OT grammar of the language that has to be learned is based on a total ranking of all the constraints. One way to look at this condition is to see it as an oversimplification that is made mainly for didactic and practical reasons. Oversimplifications may be needed to allow one to concentrate on a central problem and to sweep aside many problems that are less critical for understanding the central one (i.e. the problem of learning 'hidden' structure). Moreover, oversimplifications may be necessary to achieve interesting mathematical results that simply are not possible without them. Another way to look at this condition is to see it not as a simplification at all. Instead, it is perceived as a condition that reflects the true nature of the domain under discussion. As such the condition is a target of empirical justification.

Perhaps it is not completely clear which position Tesar and Smolensky really take with regard to the conditions under discussion: oversimplification or empirically sound restrictions:

> From the learnability perspective, the formal results given for Constraint Demotion depend critically on the assumption that the target language is given by a totally ranked hierarchy. This is a consequence of a principle implicit in CD. This principle states that the learner should assume that the description is optimal for the corresponding input, and that it is the *only* optimal description. This principle resembles other proposed learning principles, such as Clark's Principle of Contrast and Wexler's Uniqueness Principle. (Tesar & Smolensky, 2000, p. 47-48)

It appears likely to us that learning languages that do not derive from a totally ranked hierarchy is in general much more difficult than the totally ranked case. If this is indeed true, demands of learnability could ultimately explain a fundamental principle of OT: UG admits only (adult) grammars defined by totally ranked hierarchies.

---

[4] Kuhn (2003) discusses the computational consequences of such a view.

Taking the condition of total ranking as a kind of principle that indicates when language learning is simple, however, is a different idea than taking it as a strict demand on theories of learning. In our opinion, the first idea is right and the second wrong. There are many examples where the target language produces synonymies. In this vein, the consequence is to take this condition as a kind of oversimplification, the acceptance of which is justified only for doing the first significant research steps.[5]

The stochastic OT of Boersma (1998) and Boersma and Hayes (2001) is a variation of standard OT which allows for empirical coverage for many phenomena that cannot be described by assuming that the target grammar is based on one fixed total ordering of all the constraints. First at all it deals with the existence of synonymy (optionality), second it deals with the gradedness of grammaticality judgements.[6]

Following the presentation in Mattausch (2004b), we start with two major mechanical differences between stochastic OT and standard OT. Firstly, the ordinal ranking of standard OT is given up and replaced by a **continuous ranking** of the relevant constraints, each one being assigned a real number called a ranking value. The various values of the various constraints not only serve to represent the hierarchical order of the constraints (higher values meaning higher ranks), but also to measure the distance between them.

Secondly, stochastic OT employs **stochastic evaluation** in the sense that, for each individual evaluation, the value of a constraint is modified with the addition of a normal distributed noise value. It is the strict hierarchical ranking of the constraints *after* adding the noise values that is responsible for the actual evaluation of the relevant candidates. For any two constraints C_1 and C_2 whose ranking values are m and n, respectively, the actual probability that C_1 will outrank C_2 for any given evaluation is a monotonic function of the difference between their mean values m–n. On this view, a categorical ranking for two constraints C_1 » C_2 arises only when the ranking value of C_1 is high enough compared to that of C_2 and the probability of C_2 outranking C_1 is virtually nil. On the other hand, true free variation is predicted where two constraints have exactly the same ranking value. Most important however, are cases where the ranking values of two constraints are close enough to one another as to render the ranking of two constraints

---

[5] For a similar view see Anttila and Cho (1998).

[6] Boersma's stochastic OT does not make a categorical distinction between grammatical and ungrammatical expressions. Rather, it defines a possibility distribution over a set of possible expressions, assigning a degree of grammaticality.

non-categorical, but where the ranking values are not equal. In such cases, one predicts optionality without predicting totally free variation.

Aside from the advantages just described, stochastic OT has been shown to be compatible with a very powerful and elegant learning theory, namely the **Gradual Learning Algorithm** (GLA), due to Boersma (1998). The algorithm extracts a constraint ranking from a representative sample of a language. Needless to say that both GEN and the inventory of constraints have to be known in advance. Furthermore, the algorithm requires a set of pre-analyzed input-output pairs. These are pairs of phonological and phonetic representations in the realm of phonology where Boersma's system was originally developed. In the present context this amounts to form-meaning pairs $<F, M>$ as introduced in Section 1.6.

At every stage of the learning process, the algorithm has its own hypothetical **stochastic OT grammar**. When it is confronted with an observation, say a pair $<F, M>$, it generates a form F' for the observed meaning M according to its current grammar. The algorithm then compares its hypothetically generated form F' to the actual (observed) form F. If the two forms are identical, no action is taken (for the hypothetical grammar is being confirmed in such a case and does not need adjustment). If there is a mismatch though, the constraints of the learner's grammar are reranked in such a way that the observed output becomes more likely and the output that the learner produced on the basis of its hypothetical grammar becomes less likely. In particular, all constraints that favor the observation are promoted by some small predetermined value, the plasticity value, and all those that favor the errant hypothesis are demoted by that amount. This process is repeated until further observations do not lead to significant changes of the learner's grammar anymore.

Obviously, a grammar learned by this algorithm does not necessarily satisfy the test of symmetry discussed in Section 5.4. Jäger (2004) has modified the GLA such that the outcomes of this algorithm pass the test of symmetry. Jäger's bidirectional GLA can be represented schematically as the following procedure:

Initial state
All constraint values are set to 0.

Step 1: Observation
The algorithm is presented with a learning datum: a fully specified form-meaning pair $<F, M>$.

Step 2: Generation

For each constraint, a noise value is drawn from a normal distribution N and added to its current ranking. This yields a **selection point**. Constraints are ranked by descending order of the selection points. This yields a linear order of the constraints. Based on this constraint ranking, the grammar generates a hypothetical output, F', for the observed input M and a hypothetical output, M', for the observed input F.

Step 3: Comparison
If F'=F, nothing happens. Otherwise, the algorithm compares the constraint violations of the learning datum $<F, M>$ with the self-generated pair $<F'$, $M>$.
If M'=M, nothing happens. Otherwise, the algorithm compares the constraint violations of the learning datum $<F, M>$ with the self-generated pair $<F, M'>$.

Step 4: Adjustment
All constraints that favor $<F, M>$ over $<F', M>$ are increased by some small predefined numerical amount (plasticity).
All constraints that favor $<F', M>$ over $<F, M>$ are decreased by the plasticity value.
All constraints that favor $<F, M>$ over $<F, M'>$ are increased by the plasticity value.
All constraints that favor $<F, M'>$ over $<F, M>$ are decreased by the plasticity value.

Final state
Steps 1 – 4 are repeated until the constraint values stabilize.

Jäger (2004) uses this bidirectional learning algorithm to model language change. His basic idea is based on the **Iterated Learning Model** of language evolution due to Kirby and Hurford (1997). That model takes each generation of learners to be one turn in a cycle of language evolution and, by applying the learning algorithm to the output of one cycle, one may produce a second cycle, a third, a fourth, and so on (see Figure 2).

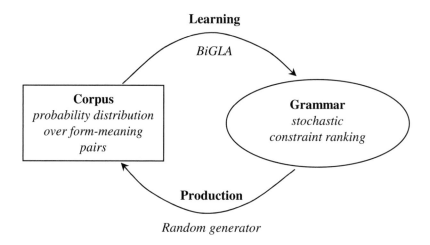

Figure 2   Jäger's bidirectional GLA within an evolutionary setting

In Jäger (2004) the working of the bidirectional GLA within the evolutionary setting was applied to Aissen's theory of differential case marking (Aissen, 2003). It could be shown that the constraint sub-hierarchies that Aissen simply assumes to be universal emerge automatically via learning if the training corpus contains substantially more harmonic meanings then disharmonic ones. Another interesting application is due to Mattausch (2004a; 2004b) who showed that very the same theory can be applied to explain the evolution of reflexive marking strategies in English and to show how an optional and infrequent marking strategy like that of Old English could evolve into a pattern of obligatory structural marking like that attested in modern English. Interestingly, the evolutionary approach can also be applied in order to give an alternative account for the children's optimal interpretation of pronouns (Section 5.6). However, we feel that even a rough discussion of this matter goes beyond the scope of this book.

5.8 Bidirectionality, Recursion, and Evolutionary Learning

At the end of this chapter, let us return to our initial question: Which conception of bidirectionality is valid, the strong one or the weak one? We have seen already that the strong mode of optimization (what we produce we are able to understand adequately and what we understand we are able to produce adequately) corresponds to the outcome of a proper mechanism of OT learning. However, the outcome of strong bidirectionality does not always correspond to the pattern displayed by adults (and children from the age of 6 or 7 on), as was shown in Sections 5.5 and 5.6. If the analyses presented in these sections, which hinge on the effect of partial blocking resulting from the mechanism of weak bidirectionality, are correct, then what is the status of weak bidirectionality?

Several people have pointed out that there seem to be problems with viewing weak bidirectionality as an on-line mechanism of linguistic competence (see Beaver and Lee, 2004; Zeevat, 2000). Beaver and Lee's main objection concerns its property of recursion, which allows for an in principle infinite number of rounds of optimization. Because suboptimal candidates can become winners in a second or later round of optimization, 'in Weak OT, everyone is a winner', as Beaver and Lee (2004: 126) put it. In other words, weak bidirectional OT's property of recursion results in an overgeneration of form-meaning pairs.

If weak bidirectional optimization is rejected as a mechanism of the grammar, however, no synchronic explanation is available for partial blocking and for the linguistic phenomena we discussed in this chapter. To be able to account for partial blocking within an OT framework without giving rise to overgeneration, Beaver and Lee (2004) propose to adopt Beaver's (2004) approach. Beaver considers a variant of weak bidirectional OT which performs only one iteration of weak bidirectionality. This effect is accomplished by incorporating a meta-constraint *Block ('A form-meaning pair may not be dominated by a bidirectionally optimal candidate in either direction of optimization in the tableau consisting of all constraints except *Block'). Incorporating such a meta-constraint, however, introduces several conceptual problems into the framework. For example, it cannot be maintained anymore that all constraints apply simultaneously, since *Block must apply after all other constraints have applied, as can be seen from the formulation of this constraint. Moreover, given the proposed formulation of *Block, the idea should be abandoned that candidates are evaluated with respect to the set of constraints independently of each other, which is one of the main characteristics of constraint application in OT.

However, we do not need to resort to conceptually problematic constraints such as *Block to solve the problem of overgeneration. There is another, perhaps more plausible, solution to the overgeneration problem. Recall that the main problem with weak bidirectional OT is that the recursion it allows for cannot apply unboundedly. This, however, does not seem to be any different from other types of recursion in natural language, for example in center embedding:

(22) The boy the girl the dog bit saw left.

This example shows that center embedding is highly restricted and results in an unmanageable form when applied twice or more. The generally adopted solution in this case is to assume that while competence allows for recursion, performance restrictions have the effect that recursion only applies a limited number of times. So we could hypothesize that weak bidirectional OT is a correct description of the competence grammar, but that the amount of recursion is limited by performance factors. This hypothesis is further supported by evidence from experiments on human reasoning. The computations humans have to perform in recursive reasoning in two-player games are highly similar to the computations involved in weak bidirectionality: They both involve the realization that the other person can have knowledge which is different from ones own knowledge, and the ability to make inferences about this knowledge by interpreting the actions (for example, uttering a certain form and not some other form, or selecting a certain move and not some other move) of the other person. In experiments on human recursive reasoning in games, it is found that human players tend to operate at only one or two levels of strategic depth (i.e., 'I think that you think...') (Hedden & Zhang, 2002). This suggests that the bounds on recursion that limit the application of weak optimization are not particular to the domain of language.

Alternatively, the conceptual problem that is raised by the existence of two notions of bidirectionality can be solved by assuming an off-line mechanism, which is based on bidirectional learning. Anton Benz worked out the formal details of such a theory (Benz, 2003). His theory is based on the idea that the speaker and hearer coordinate on form–meaning pairs which are most preferred from both perspectives. This theory predicts partial blocking as the result of an associative learning process where speaker and hearer preferences are coordinated. The whole learning process is divided into separate stages. Since this matter goes beyond the scope of this book, we refer to the original literature for the details.

Other approaches that try to ground weak bidirection in repeated process of bidirectional learning are due to van Rooy (2004), Jäger (2004), and Blutner, Borra, Lentz, Uijlings, & Zevenhuijzen (2002). It is remarkable that in this line of research the solution concept of weak bidirectionality plays an important role in describing the **direction of language change**. In fact, Horn's division of pragmatic labor (see Chapter 4) can be proven to be a consequence of weak bidirection. This observation gives substance to the claim that weak bidirection can be considered as a principle describing (in part) the direction of language change: super-optimal pairs are tentatively realized in language change. This relates to the view of Horn (1984) who considers the Q principle and the I principle as diametrically opposed forces in inference strategies of language change. The basic idea goes back to Zipf (1949), and was reconsidered in van Rooy (2004). Arguing that Horn's division of pragmatic labor is a *conventional* fact about language, this convention can be explained in terms of equilibriums of signaling games introduced by Lewis (1969) – making use of an evolutionary setting.

Concluding, the alternative suggestion is to take the weak conception of bidirectionality as a diachronic law that is grounded in recursion to learning. In addition, the alternative conception conforms to the idea that synchronic structure is significantly informed by diachronic forces. Further, it respects Zeevat's (2000) acute criticism against super-optimality as describing an online mechanism. It remains unclear, however, how the observed production/comprehension asymmetry in language acquisition discussed in Section 5.6 can be accounted for under an entirely off-line view on weak bidirectionality.

5.9 Summary

In this chapter we showed that the bidirectional perspective on optimization is intimately connected with the examination of learning. We introduced the fundamental idea of constraint demotion and discussed the bootstrap idea for learning hidden structure. In Section 5.5 and 5.6 we applied the theoretical ideas to tangible results in child language acquisition, discussing the acquisition of indefinite subject and object interpretation in Dutch and the acquisition of pronominal interpretation in English. We also discussed Paul Boersma's algorithm of gradual learning and showed how this algorithm can be modified such that its outcomes conform to the principle of strong bidirectionality. The outcomes of this bidirectional GLA algorithm do not yield the endpoint of the process of language acquisition, though. From empirical observations with respect to the two phenomena in language acquisition we discussed in this chapter, we conclude that the acquisition of adult forms and meanings requires an additional developmental step from strong bidirectionality to weak bidirectionality. This step may boil down to the ability to apply bidirectionality recursively and hence be subject to working memory limitations. An alternative foundation of weak bidirectionality was given in terms of recursive learning.

6

Foundations

6.1 Introduction

In this chapter we go into some questions concerning the interface between linguistic theory and mental representations. Optimality Theory has its source in connectionism, or parallel distributed processing, a view on cognition that emerged in the 1980s as an alternative to what is nowadays known as the classical or symbolic view.

6.2 An Architecture of Cognition

Mental representations are either conceived of as a kind of symbolic structures (language of thought) or as connectionist patterns of activation. Connectionist models are neurally inspired, computation on such a system can be called 'brain-style' computation. Basically, a connectionist approach takes something like an abstract neuron as its processing unit and computation is carried out through simple interactions among such units. The idea is that these processing units communicate by sending numbers along the lines that connect them.

The consequence of such an approach is **parallel processing** which provides a natural account of the fact that people seem to get faster, not slower, when they are able to use additional information (constraints). In a sequential machine, each additional constraint would require more time, yet parallelism deals with the multiple, simultaneous, and often mutual constraints that seem to be involved in complex processes such as language processing. Burzio (1995) argues for example that the interaction between phonology and morphology is not just one way, but mutual, which can be accounted for in a parallel model such as OT.

Another characteristic of connectionist models is that knowledge is stored in the connections between the units rather than in the units themselves. If we speak of a model's active representation at a particular time, we can associate this with the pattern of activation over the units in the system. What can be stored then are the strengths of the connections between the units so that the patterns can be recreated. This has important consequences for theories of learning as we have seen in Chapter 5. If knowledge is stored in the strengths of the interconnections between units, one might assign one unit to each pattern that is to be learned (i.e. a local representation). Another possibility is that the knowledge about an individual pattern is **distributed** over the connections among a large number of processing units.

The type of connectionist models that are at the base of Optimality Theory are Parallel Distributed Processing models (PDP) (Rumelhart, McClelland, & the PDP Research group, 1986). Let us briefly summarize some characteristics of PDP models. Specifying a PDP model begins with specifying a set of processing units and what they represent (e.g., features, words, concepts, or abstract elements over which patterns can be defined). Units represent small, featurelike entities and the pattern as a whole is the meaningful analysis. All processing is carried out by the units which receive input from their neighbors and compute an output value to send to their neighbors. The system is inherently parallel as many units carry out their computation at the same time. Three types of units are distinguished: input units, which receive input from external resources, output units, which send signals out of the system, and hidden units, which are not visible to outside systems. Associated with each unit, there is an output function which maps the current state of activation to an output signal. The pattern of activation over the set of processing units is represented by a vector: each component of the vector stands for the activation of one of the units at a certain time. Units are connected to each other. In many cases, the total input to a unit is obtained by simply multiplying the inputs from the incoming units by a weight and summing them. In that case the total pattern of connectivity can be represented by merely specifying the weights for each of the connections in the system.

From many corners it has been doubted that a connectionist model can handle complex cognitive processes such as language processing. Smolensky (1995) extensively argues, however, that symbolic and connectionist theories should be regarded as two accounts of a single cognitive system at different levels of description. He presents explicit principles for his integrated connectionist/symbolic architecture. According to him, his architecture is more than implementing one type of computation into the other. In his system, not only does symbolic computation inform the structure of connectionist networks, but also the other way around. That is, principles of connectionist computation explain and enrich symbolic theory. He illustrates this with his theory of grammar. Thus, Smolensky argues that his integrated connectionist/symbolic architecture is sufficient to explain fundamental symbolic cognitive properties such as recursivity, but moreover it is able to refine symbolic theory itself. In the next section we start with the 'sufficient part' of his claim.

6.3   Smolensky's Tensor Product Representations

This is often thought to be the fatal limitation of connectionism: the lack of a mechanism for systematically processing complex representational structures (such as sentences). One technique that has been developed to overcome that limit, is Smolensky's (1991) tensor product encoding.

The starting point of our discussion here is Van Gelder's (1990) observation that the real contrast between the symbolic approach and connectionism is not between structured as opposed to unstructured representations; rather, it is between two different ways of implementing compositional structure. Symbolic theory claims that mental representations have a combinatorial syntax and semantics, such that a representation has tokens of its constituents as literal parts. This is what Van Gelder calls **concatenative** structure: If a representation has a concatenative structure, it has an internal formal structure of a certain kind. That is, a concatenative mode of combination preserves tokens of an expression's constituents in the expression itself. It provides a way of linking or ordering constituents without altering them. A token of the symbol p standing alone is the same when appearing in the context of an expression such as $p \& q$. Van Gelder points out that almost all familiar compositional schemes are concatenative in this sense, e.g., formal languages of mathematics, logic, computer science, etc. Natural languages seem to be like that as well, at least when they are written (see, however, our Chapter 3 for more problems with this symbol preserving view of compositionality).

Standardly, according to Van Gelder, concatenative schemes are (functional) compositional, yet this does not hold the other way around. You can have merely **functional compositionality** which is obtained if it is possible to produce an expression given its constituents and also to decompose the expression back into its constituents, but the mode of combination is not concatenative. This is in fact the case for Smolensky's tensor product representations.

As was already pointed out above, in PDP models, a representation is borne by a vector. Different representations are different activity vectors over a fixed set of units, not activity over different units. If we want to embed symbolic computation in a PDP model then the question is how a vector can be treated as a symbol structure. Smolensky defines the problem as finding a mapping from a set of structured objects (for example, linguistic trees) to a vector space. This mapping should preserve the various constituency relations, such that a representation of a complex item can be generated as a combination of the representations of its parts, and those parts can be recovered if necessary. Obviously, vector addition cannot do this job. An example of vector addition:

$$
\begin{bmatrix} 1 \\ 2 \\ 3 \end{bmatrix} + \begin{bmatrix} 4 \\ 5 \\ 6 \end{bmatrix} = \begin{bmatrix} 5 \\ 7 \\ 9 \end{bmatrix}
$$

The sum of two vectors cannot be decomposed into its part again. That is, 5 could be the sum of 1 and 4, but likewise of 2 and 3, of course. Therefore, Smolensky applies the more powerful operation of **tensor product formation**. The tensor product of an n-dimensional vector **v** and an m-dimensional vector **w** is the (n×m)-dimensional vector whose values consist in all the pairwise products of the vectors **v** and **w**. An example of tensor product formation:

$$
\begin{bmatrix} 1 \\ 2 \\ 3 \end{bmatrix} \otimes \begin{bmatrix} 4 \\ 5 \end{bmatrix} = \begin{bmatrix} 4 \\ 8 \\ 12 \\ 5 \\ 10 \\ 15 \end{bmatrix}
$$

The tensor product is similar to the more familiar outer product of two vectors, except that the result is a vector rather than a matrix. Therefore, it can itself enter into vector sums and tensor products, which is important for recursivity.

Smolensky furthermore introduces the notion of role decomposition. Complex items such as linguistic structures (trees) are made up of a set of binary (left/right) branching roles with each role having a distinct filler. Two vectors representing the left and right branch roles must be linearly independent (i.e., none of them can be written as a linear combination of the others). Each branch is assigned a distinct primitive vector. Fillers are bound to the roles by the tensor product of their vectors, and the resulting tensor products are added together to obtain a single compound representation of the whole structured item. For example, if the left and right branch are represented by two independent vectors r_0 and r_1 respectively, *John* by the vector **j** and *slept* by the vector **s**, then we realize *John slept* as the vector **a** = $r_0 \otimes$**j** + $r_1 \otimes$**s**. How do we know that the resulting vector **a** actually represents *John slept* and not *Walked Bill* for example? The point is that one vector must be of the form $r_0 \otimes$**x** and the other one $r_1 \otimes$**y** and since r_0 and r_1 are independent, there is only one possibility. Similarly, a more complex structure such as *John killed Simon* can be realized as the vector **b** = $r_0 \otimes$**j** + $r_1 \otimes [r_0 \otimes$**k** + $r_1 \otimes$**s**]. So, the filler role can be extracted from the representation of the whole structure, by multiplying the overall tensor product representation by the vector corresponding to that role. Hence, the whole structure can be effectively recovered from the vectorial representation. Therefore, Smolensky's tensor product representation is functionally compositional in Van Gelder's sense.

To sum up, in this section we have shown that by tensor product encoding, complex linguistic structures can be represented in a connectionist model. As a matter of fact, tensor product representation is not the only way to encode linguistic constituent structure. Another popular way is Recursive Auto-Associative Memory (RAAM) (Pollack, 1990) or fixed width vector representations (Plate, 2000). These alternatives are both discussed in Smolensky and Legendre (2005). In this section we concentrated on Smolensky's claim that fundamental symbolic properties of language can be adequately captured within his integrated connectionist/symbolic architecture by using tensor product formation. The next section is dedicated to Smolensky's claim that, moreover, connectionist principles are in fact essential to a theory that can account for certain fundamental properties of language and grammar.

6.4   Harmonic Grammar – OT's Predecessor

Optimality Theory has become a popular trend in linguistics after its introduction in 1993 by Alan Prince and Paul Smolensky. The most revolutionary innovation in OT was the fact that the constraints are soft which means that an output can still be grammatical if constraints are violated. Violations have to be minimal, however, such that a constraint may be violated, but only in order to satisfy a higher ranked constraint. The fact that the well-formedness constraints in OT are soft and potentially conflicting is a direct consequence of principles of connectionist computation. As such, Smolensky views it as the manifestation of one of the basic principles of his cognitive architecture that integrates symbolic and connectionist principles, being that not all important higher cognitive processes are described by symbolic algorithms.

In OT as well as in its predecessor Harmonic Grammar (Smolensky, 1986; 1995) the linguistic notion of well-formedness and a connectionist notion of **well-formedness** or **Harmony** are brought together. In a connectionist network, the Harmony of an activation pattern is a number that measures the degree to which the pattern is well-formed according to the connections in the network. Let us illustrate this by a simple example (see Figure 1 below).

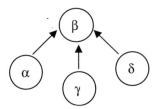

Figure 1 A connectionist network

Suppose that in the above network the weight value of the connection from unit α to unit β is negative, e.g., $w_{\beta\alpha} = -5$. Such a connection can be interpreted as a constraint: if α is active, then β should not be active. Similarly, the connection from γ to β can be interpreted as a constraint. Suppose this one is positive, e.g., $w_{\beta\gamma} = +3$. Suppose that α and γ are equally active at the same time, then β is subject to two conflicting constraints. The prediction is then that the strongest constraint will win, in this example the negative one, which has a higher weight value. This means that the network will create an activation pattern that violates the positive constraint in order to satisfy the negative constraint. Such an activation pattern has maximal Harmony with respect to the two connections considered here. However, if the connection from δ to β is positive as well with $w_{\beta\delta} = +3$ and δ is also equally active at the same time, then the cumulative effect of $w_{\beta\delta}$ and $w_{\beta\gamma}$ will overrule the negative $w_{\beta\alpha}$.

In this respect, Harmonic Grammar as a numerical theory that centers around the concept of Harmony, crucially differs from its non-numerical counterpart Optimality Theory, a theory that deals with strict dominance hierarchies of constraints instead of weight values. In Optimality Theory no number of weaker constraints can override a stronger constraint. That is, each constraint is stronger than all weaker constraints combined. In Harmonic Grammar, on the other hand, we do find effects of cumulativity. Two weaker constraints combined can override one stronger constraint. Also, the degree of activation of the constraints matters. The Harmony of an activation pattern is computed on the basis of the weight values between the units as well as the activation values of the units. Thus, if two constraints compete and one is weaker than the other yet activated to a higher degree, this one can still win.

In general, the process of **Harmony maximization** (or parallel soft constraint satisfaction) applies to the complete set of connections in a network. The total Harmony of a pattern x in a network with connection weight matrix **W** is the sum of the Harmony values of x with respect to all the individual connections:

$$H(x) = \sum_{\beta\alpha} H_{\beta\alpha} = \sum_{\beta\alpha} a_\beta \, w_{\beta\alpha} \, a_\alpha$$

As the network computes a completion **x** of an input, part of what it is doing is mapping the input to a corresponding output. We can think of this as a grammatical function which maps an input to an output. The activation settles to a final vector which maximizes Harmony, that is, for which the pair <input, output> is optimal.

Harmony maximization is an essential theorem in Smolensky's theory: the net effect of processing in a network is to complete the input pattern into a total activation pattern with maximal Harmony. No pattern is unacceptable because it violates too many constraints. A pattern is rejected for one reason only: there is a better one. This can be considered the optimal parse according to the grammar encoded in the network's connections. A symbolic version of the theorem is formulated by Smolensky (1995: 256) as follows:

> Given an input symbolic structure *i*, the Harmonic Grammar assigns to *i* the output symbolic structure ('parse') *s* with maximal Harmony, among those which are completions of *i*. The higher the value of Harmony of this parse structure *s*, the more well-formed the grammar judges the input.

It will be clear that this latter principle (the higher the Harmony value, the more well-formed the input) explains the possibility of gradual grammaticality judgments. For instance, we might hypothesize that the Harmony value 0 (zero) leads to a grammaticality judgment '?' for the input. Given the strengths (or in OT the ranking) of the constraints, not only the optimal output but also the nearly optimal alternatives can be predicted.

In a case study of French unaccusatives, Legendre et al. (1990a; 1990b) account for relative well-formedness as well as gradual unaccusativity, that is the fact that some verbs appear to be 'more unaccusative' than others when subject to syntactic and semantic tests that supposedly distinguish between unergative and unaccusative verbs. Instead of using hard conditions and a strict distinction between unaccusative and unergative intransitives, the connectionist approach of Legendre et al. offers the possibility of formalizing both syntactic and semantic **tendencies** or **preferences** as soft constraints.

As pointed out above, Optimality Theory is the non-numerical successor of Harmonic Grammar. Why Prince and Smolensky (1993) proposed this shift from numerical to non-numerical constraint satisfaction, is explained by Smolensky (1995: 266) as follows: 'Phonological applications of Harmonic Grammar led Alan Prince and myself to a remarkable discovery: in a broad set of cases, at least, the relative strengths of constraints *need not be specified numerically*. For if the numerically weighted constraints needed in these cases are ranked from strongest to weakest, it turns out that each constraint is stronger than all the weaker constraints *combined*.' In other words, the shift from Harmonic Grammar to Optimality Theory appears to be mainly motivated by empirical findings in the domain of phonology. Prince and Smolensky (1997) also claim that the shift is empirically motivated:

> The key observation is this: In a variety of clear cases where there is a strength asymmetry between two conflicting constraints, no amount of success on the weaker constraint can compensate for failure on the stronger one. (…) Extending this observation leads to the hypothesis that grammar consists entirely of constraints arranged in a strict domination hierarchy (…)

So, the shift to Optimality Theory was mainly empirically motivated. One other possible advantage of strict dominance lies in the robustness of processing, following a suggestion of David Rumelhart in Smolensky (1995, note 38: 286):

> Suppose it is important for communication that language processing computes global harmony maxima fairly reliably, so different speakers are not constantly computing idiosyncratic parses which are various local Harmony maxima. Then this puts a (meta-)constraint on the Harmony function: it must be such that local maximization algorithms give global maxima with reasonably high probability. Strict domination of grammatical constraints appears to satisfy this (meta-)constraint.

So, the main motivation that favors OT over Harmonic Grammar is empirical and based on data found originally in the domain of phonology. However, the one and only application of Harmonic Grammar was situated in the domain of syntax and semantics (Legendre et al., 1990a, 1990b). Moreover, recent work by Jäger and Rosenbach (2004) strongly suggests that cumulativity effects are obtained in empirical data in the domain of syntax and semantics. On the basis of this, they draw the conclusion that probabilistic harmonic grammars do in fact a better job in modeling grammatical variation in syntax and semantics than a probabilistic version of 'standard' OT.

Presently, it is rather unclear how to give a theoretically satisfying account that explains under which conditions the strict domination of constraints applies and under which conditions it does not. In our opinion, this is a very important problem, that relates to the old dictum that 'Grammar does not count'. In the words of Bechtel, the solution to this problem

> (…) may create a rapprochement between network models and symbolic accounts that triggers an era of dramatic progress in which alignments are found and used all the way from the neural level to the cognitive/linguistic level (Bechtel, 2002).

6.5 Summary

In this chapter we have discussed the fundamental question whether Optimality Theory provides a way of integrating the subsymbolic level of the brain with the symbolic level that seems necessary for the description and explanation of cognitive processes.

Summing up, we believe that Optimality Theory has proposed a new computational architecture for cognition which claims to integrate connectionist and symbolic computation. Though too simple to give a full justification of OT's basic principles, the presented ideas of unifying connectionism and symbolism can help to understand them. In our opinion, it is important to get an active dialogue between the traditional approaches to semantics and pragmatics and their embodiment in a neural network architecture. Perhaps, this dialogue may stimulate the present discussion of founding the basic principles of Optimality Theory, and likewise it may shed new light on old notions like compositionality, partiality, underspecification, prototypicality, pragmatic enrichment, presumptive meaning, modularity, and the systematicity of language.

References

Ackema, P., & Neeleman, A. 1998. Optimal questions. *Natural Language & Linguistic Theory* 16: 443-490.

Aissen, J. 2003. Differential Object Marking: Iconicity vs. Economy. *Natural Language and Linguistic Theory* 21: 435-483.

Anttila, A., & Cho, Y.-M. Y. 1998. Variation and change in Optimality Theory. *Lingua* 104: 31-56.

Anttila, A., & Fong, V. 2000. The Partitive Constraint in Optimality Theory. *Journal of Semantics* 17: 281-314.

Archangeli, D. 1997. Optimality Theory: An Introduction to Linguistics in the 1990s. In D. Archangeli & D. T. Langendoen (Eds.), *Optimality Theory. An Overview*, 1-32. Malden, MA/Oxford, UK: Blackwell.

Archangeli, D., & Langendoen, D. T. 1997. *Optimality theory: An overview*. Malden, MA/Oxford, UK: Blackwell.

Aronoff, M. 1976. *Word Formation in Generative Grammar*. Cambridge MA: MIT Press.

Asher, N., & Lascarides, A. 1998. Bridging. *Journal of Semantics* 15: 83-113.

Atlas, J. D., & Levinson, S. C. 1981. It-clefts, informativeness and logical form. In P. Cole (Ed.), *Radical Pragmatics*, 1-61. New York: Academic Press.

Barsalou, L. W., Yeh, W., Luka, B. J., Olseth, K. L., Mix, K. S., & Wu, L.-L. 1995. Concepts and meaning. In K. Beals & G. Cooke & D. Kathman & K. E. McCullough & S. Kita & D. Testen (Eds.), *Chicago Linguistics Society 29: Papers from the parasession on conceptual representations*, 23-61: University of Chicago: Chicago Linguistics Society.

Bartsch, R. 1987. Context-dependent interpretations of lexical items. In R. Bartsch & J. van Benthem & P. van Emde-Boas (Eds.), *Semantics and contextual expressions*. Dordrecht: Foris.

Beaver, D. 2004. The optimization of discourse anaphora. *Linguistics and Philosophy* 27(1): 3-56.

Beaver, D., & Lee, H. 2004. Input-output mismatches in OT. In R. Blutner and H. Zeevat (Eds.), *Optimality Theory and Pragmatics*. Houndmills, Basingstoke, Hampshire/New York: Palgrave/Macmillan.

Bechtel, W. 2002. *Connectionism and the Mind*. Oxford: Blackwell.

Benz, A. 2003. Partial Blocking, associative learning, and the principle of weak optimality. In J. Spenader & A. Eriksson & Ö. Dahl (Eds.), *Proceedings of the Stockholm Workshop on Variation within Optimality Theory*, 150-159. Stockholm.

Bergsma-Klein, W. 1996. *Specificity in child Dutch: An experimental study*. Unpublished MA thesis, Utrecht University.

Bloom, P., Barss, A., Nicol, J., & Conway, L. 1994. Children's knowledge of binding and coreference: Evidence from spontaneous speech. *Language* 70(1): 53-71.

Blutner, R. 1998. Lexical pragmatics. *Journal of Semantics* 15: 115-162.

Blutner, R. 2000. Some aspects of optimality in natural language interpretation. *Journal of Semantics* 17: 189-216.

Blutner, R. 2002. Lexical semantics and pragmatics. *Linguistische Berichte* 10: 27-58.

Blutner, R. 2004. Pragmatics and the lexicon. In L. Horn & G. Ward (Eds.), *Handbook of pragmatics*. Oxford: Blackwell.

Blutner, R., Borra, E., Lentz, T., Uijlings, A., & Zevenhuijzen, R. 2002. Signalling games: Hoe evolutie optimale strategieen selecteert, *Handelingen van de 24ste Nederlands-Vlaamse Filosofiedag*. Amsterdam: Universiteit van Amsterdam.

Blutner, R., Hendriks, P., & de Hoop, H. 2003. *A new hypothesis on compositionality*. In: P. Szlezak (Ed.) *Proceedings of the Joint International Conference on Cognitive Science*, 53-57. Sydney: ICCS/ASCS

Blutner, R., & Zeevat, H. 2004. Editor's Introduction: Pragmatics in Optimality Theory. In R. Blutner & H. Zeevat (Eds.), *Optimality Theory and Pragmatics*. Houndmills, Basingstoke, Hampshire: Palgrave/Macmillan.

Boersma, P. 1998. *Functional phonology*. The Hague: Holland Academic Graphics.

Boersma, P., & Hayes, B. 2001. Empirical tests of the gradual learning algorithm. *Linguistic Inquiry* 32: 45-86.

Bransford, J. D., Barklay, J. R., & Franks, J. J. 1982. Sentence memory: A constructive versus interpretive approach. *Cognitive Psychology* 3: 193-209.

Bresnan, J. 1973. The syntax of the comparative clause construction in English. *Linguistic Inquiry* 4: 275-343.

Buchwald, A., Schwartz, O., Seidl, A., & Smolensky, P. 2002. Recoverability optimality theory: Discourse anaphora in a bidirectional framework. In: *Proceedings of the sixth workshop on the semantics and pragmatics of dialogue* (EDILOG 2002), Edinburgh, UK.

Burzio, L. 1995. The rise of optimality theory. *Glot International* 1(6): 3-7.

Burzio, L. 1998. Anaphora and soft constraints. In P. Barbosa & D. Fox & P. Hagstrom & M. McGinnis & D. Pesetsky (Eds.), *Is the best good enough?* Cambridge, Mass.: The MIT Press.

Carston, R. 2002. *Thoughts and Utterances: The Pragmatics of Explicit Communication*. Oxford: Blackwell.

Carston, R. 2003. Explicature and semantics. In S. David & B. Gillon (Eds.), *Semantics: A Reader*. Oxford: Oxford University Press.

Carston, R. 2004. Relevance theory and the saying/implicating distinction. In L. Horn & G. Ward (Eds.), *Handbook of Pragmatics* (pp. 633-656). Oxford: Blackwell.

Chien, Y.-C., & Wexler, K. 1990. Children's knowledge of locality conditions on binding as evidence for the modularity of syntax and pragmatics. *Language Acquisition* 13: 225-295.

Choi, H.-W. 1996. *Optimizing structure in context*. Unpublished PhD thesis, Stanford University.

Chomsky, N. 1981. *Lectures on government and binding*. Dordrecht: Foris.

Chomsky, N. 1995. *The Minimalist Program*. Cambridge MA: MIT Press.

Clark, H. H., & Clark, E. V. 1977. *Psychology and Language. An introduction to Psycholinguistics*. New York, Chicago, San Francisco, Atlanta: Harcourt Brace Jovanovich.

Cole, P. (Ed.). (1981). *Radical pragmatics*. New York: Academic Press.

Comrie, B. 1989. *Language Universals and Linguistic Typology*. Chicago: University of Chicago Press.

Dalrymple, M., Shieber, S. M., & Pereira, F. 1991. Ellipsis and Higher-Order Unification. *Linguistics and Philosophy* 14: 399-452.

de Hoop, H. 1996. *Case Configuration and Noun Phrase Interpretation*. New York & London: Garland Publishing.

de Hoop, H. 2000. Optimal scrambling and interpretation. In H. Bennis & M. Everaert & E. Reuland (Eds.), *Interface Strategies*, 153-168. Amsterdam: KNAW.

de Hoop, H. 2003. Scrambling in Dutch: Optionality and Optimality. In S. Karimi (Ed.), *Word Order and Scrambling*, 201-216. Oxford: Blackwell.

de Hoop, H., & Solà, J. 1996. Determiners, Context Sets, and Focus. In: J. Camacho, L. Choueiri, & M. Wantanebe (Eds.) *The proceedings of the Fourteenth West Coast Conference on Formal Linguistics*. Stanford: CSLI

de Hoop, H., & de Swart, H. E. 2000. Temporal adjunct clauses in optimality theory. *Rivista di Linguistica* 12(1): 107-127.

de Hoop, H., & Krämer, I. M. to appear. Children's optimal interpretations of indefinite subjects and objects. *Language Acquisition*

de Hoop, H., & de Swart, P. 2004. Contrast in Discourse. Guest Editors' Introduction. *Journal of Semantics*. 21: 87-93

de Swart, H. E. 1999. Position and meaning: time adverbials in context. In P. Bosch & R. van der Sandt (Eds.), *Focus: linguistic, cognitive and computational perspectives*, 336-361. Cambridge: Cambridge University Press.

Dekker, P., & van Rooy, R. 2000. Bi-Directional Optimality Theory: An Application of Game Theory. *Journal of Semantics* 17: 217-242.

Dowty, D. 1979. *Word meaning and Montague grammar. The semantics of verbs and times in Generative Semantics and in Montague's PTQ*. Dordrecht: Reidel.

Ducrot, O. 1972. *Dire et ne pas dire. Principes de sémantique linguistique*. Paris: Hermann.

Dugdale, N., & Lowe, C. F. 2000. Testing for symmetry in the conditional discriminations of language-trained chimpanzees. *Journal of the Experimental Analysis of Behavior* 73(1): 5-22.

Engdahl, E. 1983. Parasitic gaps. *Linguistics and Philosophy* 6: 5-34.

Farmer, A. K., & Harnish, R. M. 1987. Communicative reference with pronouns. In J. Verschueren & M. Bertucelli-Papi (Eds.), *The pragmatic perspective*. Amsterdam: John Benjamins.

Gawron, J. M. 1995. Comparatives, Superlatives, and Resolution. *Linguistics and Philosophy* 18: 333-380.

Gazdar, G. 1979. *Pragmatics*. New York: Academic Press.

Geis, M., & Zwicky, A. 1971. On invited inference. *Linguistic Inquiry* 2: 561-579.

Geurts, B. 2000. Buoyancy and Strength. *Journal of Semantics* 17: 315-333.

Gibson, E., & Wexler, K. 1994. Triggers. *Linguistic Inquiry* 25: 407-454.

Givón, T. 1983. Introduction. In T. Givón (Ed.), *Topic Continuity in Discourse: A quantitative cross-language study*, 5-41. Amsterdam: John Benjamins.

Green, G. 1990. Differences in development of visual and auditory-visual equivalence relations. *Journal of the Experimental Analysis of Behavior* 51: 385-392.

Grice, P. 1975. Logic and conversation. In P. Cole & J. L. Morgan (Eds.), *Syntax and Semantics, 3: Speech Acts*, 41-58. New York: Academic Press.

Grice, P. 1989. *Studies in the way of words*. Cambridge Mass.: Harvard University Press.

Grimshaw, J. 1987. Subdeletion. *Linguistic Inquiry* 18: 659-669.

Grimshaw, J. 1997. Projection, heads, and optimality. *Linguistic Inquiry* 28: 373-422.

Grimshaw, J., & Rosen, S. T. 1990. Knowledge and obedience: The developmental status of the binding theory. *Linguistic Inquiry* 21: 187-222.

Grimshaw, J., & Samek-Lodovici, V. 1998. Optimal subjects and subject universals. In P. Barbosa & D. Fox & P. Hagstrom & M. McGinnis & D. Pestsky (Eds.), *Is the Best Good Enough? Optimality and Competition in Syntax*, 193-219. Cambridge, MA: MIT Press.

Grodzinsky, Y., & Reinhart, T. 1993. The innateness of binding and the development of coreference. *Linguistic Inquiry* 24: 69-101.

Hedden, T., & Zhang, J. 2002. What do you think I think you think? Strategic reasoning in matrix games. *Cognition* 85: 1-36.

Heim, I. 1982. *The semantics of definite and indefinite noun phrases*. Ph.D. thesis, Amherst, MA: GLSA

Heinämäki, O. 1978. *Semantics of English temporal connectives*. Unpublished PhD thesis, University of Texas, Austin.

Hendriks, P., & de Hoop, H. 1997. On the interpretation of semantic relations in the absence of syntactic structure. In: P. Dekker, M. Stokhof, & Y. Venema (Eds.) *The Proceedings of the 11th Amsterdam Colloquium*. Amsterdam: ILLC

Hendriks, P., & de Hoop, H. 2001. Optimality theoretic semantics. *Linguistics and Philosophy* 24: 1-32.

Hendriks, P., & Spenader, J. 2004. A bidirectional explanation of the pronoun interpretation problem. In: P. Schlenker & E. Keenan (Eds.), *Proceedings of the ESSLLI'04 Workshop on Semantic Approaches to Binding Theory*. Nancy.

Hendriks, P., & Spenader, J. in preparation. When production precedes comprehension: An optimization approach to the acquisition of pronouns.

Hintikka, J. 1983. *The game of language. Studies in game-theoretical semantics and its applications*. Dordrecht: Reidel.

Hobbs, J., Stickel, M. E., Appelt, D. E., & Martin, P. 1993. Interpretation as abduction. *Artificial Intelligence* 63: 69-142.

Hobbs, J. R., & Kehler, A. 1997. A Theory of Parallelism and the Case of VP Ellipsis. In: P.R. Cohen, & W. Wahlster (Eds.), *Proceedings of the 35th Annual Meeting of the Association for Computational Linguistics*, 394-401. Madrid: Association for Computational Linguistics.

Horn, L. 1984. Towards a new taxonomy of pragmatic inference: Q-based and R-based implicature. In D. Schiffrin (Ed.), *Meaning, form, and use in con-*

text: Linguistic applications, 11-42. Washington: Georgetown University Press.

Horn, L. 1989. *A natural history of negation*. Chicago: Chicago University Press.

Horn, L. 2000. From if to iff: conditional perfection as pragmatic strengthening. *Journal of Pragmatics* 32: 289-326.

Householder, F. W. 1971. *Linguistic Speculations*. London and New York: Cambridge University Press.

Jackendoff, R. 1983. *Semantics and Cognition*. Cambridge, Mass.: MIT Press.

Jäger, G. 1997. *Anaphora and Ellipsis in Type-Logical Grammar*. Paper presented at the Eleventh Amsterdam Colloquium, Amsterdam.

Jäger, G. 2002. Some notes on the formal properties of bidirectional optimality theory. *Journal of Logic, Language and Information* 11: 427-451.

Jäger, G. 2004. Learning constraint sub-hierarchies. The bidirectional gradual learning Algorithm. In R. Blutner & H. Zeevat (Eds.), *Pragmatics and Optimality Theory*. Houndmills, Basingstoke, Hampshire: Palgrave Macmillan.

Jäger, G., & Rosenbach, A. (2004). *The winner takes it all - almost. Cumulativity in grammatical variation*. Unpublished manuscript, Potsdam & Düsseldorf.

Jakubowicz, C. 1991. *Binding principles and acquisition fact revisited*. Paper presented at the 21st Annual Meeting of the North East Linguistics Society (NELS), Amherst: University of Massachusetts.

Johnson-Laird, P. N. 1981. Mental models of meaning. In A. K. Joshi, B. L. Webber, I.A. Sag (Eds.), *Elements of Discourse Understanding*, 106-126. Cambridge: Cambridge University Press.

Johnson-Laird, P. N. 1983. *Mental models: Towards a cognitive science of language, inference, and consciousness*. Cambridge: Cambridge University Press.

Johnson-Laird, P. N. 1988. How is meaning mentally represented? In U. S. Eco, M. Santambrogio, P. Violi (Eds.), *Meaning and mental representation*, 99-118. Bloomington: Indiana University Press.

Kager, R. 1999. *Optimality theory*. Cambridge: Cambridge University Press.

Kamp, H. 1981. A theory of truth and semantic representation. In J. Groenendijk, T. Janssen, & M. Stokhof (Eds.), *Formal methods in the study of language*. Amsterdam: Mathematisch Centrum.

Kaplan, D. 1979. On the logic of demonstratives. *Journal of Philosophical Logic* 8: 81-89.

Kennedy, C. 1997. *Projecting the Adjective: The Syntax and Semantics of Gradability and Comparison*. Unpublished PhD Thesis, University of California, Santa Cruz.

Kennedy, C. 2002. Comparative deletion and optimality in syntax. *Natural Language & Linguistic Theory* 20: 553-621.

Kintsch, W. 1974. *The Representation of Meaning in Memory.* Hillsdale, New Jersey: Erlbaum.

Kiparsky, P. 1983. *Word-formation and the lexicon.* Proceedings of the 1982 Mid-America Linguistic Conference, Kansas.

Kirby, S., & Hurford, J. (1997). *The evolution of incremental learning: language, development and critical periods.* Edinburgh: University of Edinburgh.

Koster, C. 1993. *Errors in Anaphora Acquisition.* Unpublished Ph.D. Dissertation, Utrecht University, Utrecht.

Krahmer, E., & van Deemter, K. 1997. Presuppositions as anaphors: Towards a full understanding of partial matches. In P. Dekker, J. van der Does & H. de Hoop (Eds.), *De Dag. Proceedings of the Workshop on Definites.* Utrecht: Utrecht Institute of Linguistics, OTS.

Krämer, I. M. 2000. *Interpreting Indefinites. An experimental study of children's language comprehension.* Unpublished PhD thesis, Utrecht University.

Kuhn, J. 2003. *Optimality-Theoretic Syntax - A Declarative Approach.* Stanford, CA: CSLI Publications.

Lascarides, A., & Asher, N. 1993. Temporal interpretation, discourse relations and commonsense entailment. *Linguistics and Philosophy* 16: 437-493.

Lascarides, A., Briscoe, T., Asher, N., & Copestake, A. 1995. Order independent and persistent typed default unification. *Linguistics and Philosophy* 19: 1-90.

Laurence, S., & Margolis, E. 1999. Concepts and cognitive science. In E. Margolis & S. Laurence (Eds.), *Concepts. Core Readings,* 3-81. Cambridge, MA; London, GB: The MIT Press.

Lee, H. 2003. Parallel Optimization in Case Systems. In M. Butt & T. King (Eds.), *Nominals: Inside and Out.* Stanford: CSLI.

Legendre, G. 2001. Introduction to Optimality Theory in Syntax. In G. Legendre & J. Grimshaw & S. Vikner (Eds.), *Optimality-Theoretic Syntax,* 1-27. Cambridge, MA: MIT Press.

Legendre, G., Miyata, Y., & Smolensky, P. 1990a. Harmonic grammar - A formal multi-level connectionist theory of linguistic well-formedness: Theoretical foundations. *Proceedings of the Twelfth Annual Meeting of the Cognitive Science Society.*

Legendre, G., Miyata, Y., & Smolensky, P. 1990b. Harmonic grammar - A formal multi-level connectionist theory of linguistic well-formedness: An application. *Proceedings of the Twelfth Annual Meeting of the Cognitive Science Society.*

Levinson, S. 1983. *Pragmatics.* Cambridge: CUP.

Levinson, S. 1987. Pragmatics and the grammar of anaphora. *Journal of Linguistics* 23: 379-434.

Levinson, S. 2000. *Presumptive meaning: The theory of generalized conversational implicature*. Cambridge, Mass.: MIT Press.

Lewis, D. 1969. *Convention: A Philosophical Study*. Princeton: Harvard University Press.

Logan, G. D. 1988. Toward an instance theory of automatization. *Psychological Review* 95: 492-527.

Mann, W., & Thompson, S. 1988. Rhetorical structure theory: towards a functional theory of text organization. *TEXT* 8: 243-281.

Margolis, E., & Laurence, S. 1999. *Concepts. Core Readings*. Cambridge, MA; London, GB: The MIT Press.

Matsumoto, Y. 1995. The conversational condition on Horn scales. *Linguistics and Philosophy* 18: 21-60.

Mattausch, J. 2004a. Optimality Theoretic Pragmatics and Binding Phenomena. In R. Blutner & H. Zeevat (Eds.), *Optimality Theory and Pragmatics*. Houndmills, Basingstoke, Hampshire: Palgrave/Macmillan.

Mattausch, J. 2004b. *On the Optimization & Grammaticalization of Anaphora*. Unpublished Ph.D. Thesis, Humboldt University, Berlin.

McCarthy, J. 1980. Circumscription - A Form of Non-Monotonic Reasoning. *Artificial Intelligence* 13: 27-39.

McCarthy, J., & Prince, A. 1993. Prosodic Morphology I: Constraint Interaction and Satisfaction. Unpublished manuscript, available as ROA 482-1201.

McCawley, J. D. 1978. Conversational implicature and the lexicon. In P. Cole (Ed.), *Syntax and Semantics 9: Pragmatics*, 245-259. New York: Academic Press.

McCawley, J. D. 1998. *The Syntactic Phenomena of English*. 2nd ed. Chicago: The University of Chicago Press.

Merchant, J. 2001. *The syntax of silence: Sluicing, islands, and the theory of ellipsis*. Oxford: Oxford University Press.

Merin, A. 1999. Information, relevance, and social decision making: Some principles and results of decision-theoretic semantics. In L. S. Moss & J. Ginzburg & M. d. Rijke (Eds.), *Logic, Language, and Computation*. vol. II. Stanford, Cal.: CSLI Publications.

Misker, J. M. V., & Anderson, J. R. 2003. Combining Optimality Theory and a Cognitive Architecture, *the European Conference on Cognitive Modeling 2003*. Bamberg, Germany.

Montague, R. 1970. Universal grammar. *Theoria* 36: 373-398.

Morrill, G. 1994. *Type Logical Grammar. Categorial Logic of Signs*. Dordrecht: Kluwer.

Murphy, G. L. 1985. Processes of Understanding Anaphora. *Journal of Memory and Language* 24: 290-303.

Neeleman, A., & Reinhart, T. 1998. Scrambling and the PF interface. In W. Geuder & M. Butt (Eds.), *The Projection of Arguments: Lexical and compositional factors*, 309-353. Stanford: CSLI.

Nunberg, G. 1979. The non-uniqueness of semantic solutions: Polysemy. *Linguistics and Philosophy* 3: 143-184.

Nunberg, G. 1995. Transfers of meaning. *Journal of Semantics* 12: 109-132.

Osherson, D., & Smith, E. 1981. On the adequacy of prototype theory as a theory of concepts. *Cognition* 9: 35-58.

Partee, B. 1973. Some structural analogies between tenses and pronouns in English. *Journal of Philosophy* 70: 601-609.

Partee, B. 1984. Nominal and temporal anaphora. *Linguistics and Philosophy* 7: 243-286.

Pesetsky, D. 1998. Some Optimality Principles of Sentence Pronunciation. In P. Barbosa, D. Fox, P. Hagstrom & M. McGinnis & D. Pesetsky (Eds.), *Is the best good enough?*, 337-383. Cambridge, MA: MIT Press.

Pinkal, M. 1995. *Logic and Lexicon. The Semantics of the Indefinite*. Dordrecht: Kluwer.

Pinkham, J. 1982. *The Formation of Comparative Clauses in French and English*. Bloomington, Indiana: Indiana University Linguistics Club.

Plate, T. A. 2000. Analogy retrieval and processing with distributed vector representations. *Expert Systems: The International Journal of Knowledge Engineering and Neural Networks* 17(1, Special Issue on Connectionist Symbol Processing): 29-40.

Pollack, J. B. 1990. Recursive distributed representations. *Artificial Intelligence* 46(1-2): 77-105.

Prince, A., & Smolensky, P. 1991. Notes on Connectionism and Harmony Theory in Linguistics, *Technical Report*: Department of Computer Science, University of Colorado, Boulder.

Prince, A., & Smolensky, P. 1993. *Optimality theory: Constraint Interaction in Generative Grammar*. Rutgers Center for Cognitive Science: Technical Report RuCCSTR-2. Published in 1993 by Malden, MA: Blackwell.

Prince, A., & Smolensky, P. 1997. Optimality Theory: From Neural Networks to Universal Grammar. *Science* 275: 1604-1610.

Prüst, H. 1992. *On Discourse Structuring, VP Anaphora and Gapping*. Unpublished PhD thesis, University of Amsterdam, Amsterdam.

Quine, W. 1951/1980. Two dogmas of empiricism, *From a logical point of view: Nine logico-philosophical essays*, 20-46. Cambridge, MA: Harvard University Press.

Rayner, M., & Banks, A. 1990. An Implementable Semantics for Comparative Constructions. *Computational Linguistics* 16(2): 86-112.

Reinhart, T. 1983. Coreference and bound anaphora: A restatement of the anaphora questions. *Linguistics and Philosophy* 6: 47-88.

Reinhart, T., & Reuland, E. 1993. Reflexivity. *Linguistic Inquiry* 24: 657-720.

Rooth, M. 1985. *Association with Focus*. PhD thesis. Amherst, MA: GLSA.

Rumelhart, D. E., & McClelland, J., & PDP Research Group. 1986. *Parallel Distributed Processing. Explorations in the Microstructure of Cognition.* Cambridge, MA: MIT Press.

Sag, I. 1981. Formal semantics and extralinguistic context. In P. Cole (Ed.), *Radical Pragmatics*, 273-294. New York: Academic Press.

Sag, I., & Hankamer, J. 1984. Towards a Theory of Anaphoric Processing. *Linguistics and Philosophy* 7: 325-345.

Savage-Rumbaugh, E. S. 1984. Acquisition of functional symbol usage in apes and children. In H. L. Roitblat & T. G. Bever & H. S. Terrace (Eds.), *Animal Cognition*, 291-310. Hillsdale, NJ: Lawrence Erlbaum Associates.

Savage-Rumbaugh, S., & Lewin, R. 1994. *Kanzi: The Ape at the Brink of the Human Mind.* John Wiley & Sons.

Shoham, Y. 1988. *Reasoning about Change.* Cambridge, Mass: MIT Press.

Smolensky, P. 1986. Information Processing in Dynamical Systems: Foundations of Harmony Theory. In D. E. Rumelhart & J. McClelland & PDP Research Group (Eds.), *Parallel Distributed Processing. Explorations in the microstructure of Cognition.* vol. 1. Cambridge, MA: MIT Press.

Smolensky, P. 1991. Connectionism, Constituency, and the Language of Thought. In B. Loewer & G. Rey (Eds.), *Meaning in Mind. Fodor and his Critics*, 201-333. Oxford, UK & Cambridge, MA: Blackwell.

Smolensky, P. 1995. Constituent structure and explanation in an integrated connectionist/symbolic cognitive architecture. In C. Macdonald & G. Macdonald (Eds.), *Connectionism: Debates on Psychological Explanation*, 221-290. Oxford: Blackwell.

Smolensky, P. 1996. On the comprehension/production dilemma in child language. *Linguistic Inquiry* 27: 720-731.

Smolensky, P., & Legendre, G. 2005. *The Harmonic Mind: form neural computation to optimality-theoretic grammar.* Oxford: Blackwell.

Smyth, R. 1994. Grammatical Determinants of Ambiguous Pronoun Resolution. *Journal of Psycholinguistic Research* 23(3): 197-229.

Snyder, W., Wexler, K., & Das, D. 1995. *The Syntactic Representation of Degree and Quantity: Perspectives from Japanese and Child English.* Paper presented at the West Coast Conference on Formal Linguistics XIII, Stanford.

Speas, M. 1997. Optimality Theory and Syntax: Null Pronouns and Control. In D. Archangeli & D. T. Langendoen (Eds.), *Optimality Theory. An Overview*, 171-199. Malden, MA/Oxford, UK: Blackwell.

Sperber, D., & Wilson, D. 1986. *Relevance.* Oxford: Basil Blackwell.

Tanenhaus, M., & Carlson, G. 1990. Comprehension of Deep and Surface Verbphrase Anaphors. *Language and Cognitive Processes* 5(4): 257-280.

ter Meulen, A. G. B. 2000. Optimal Reflexivity in Dutch. *Journal of Semantics* 17: 263-280.

Termeer, M. 2002. *"Een meisje ging twee keer van de glijbaan."* A study of indefinite subject NPs in child language. Unpublished MA thesis, Utrecht.

Tesar, B., & Smolensky, P. 1998. Learnability in Optimality Theory. *Linguistic Inquiry* 29: 229-268.

Tesar, B., & Smolensky, P. 2000. *Learnability in optimality theory*. Cambridge Mass.: MIT Press.

van der Does, J., & de Hoop, H. 1998. Type-shifting and scrambled definites. *Journal of Semantics* 15: 393-416.

Van Gelder, T. 1990. Compositionality: a connectionist variation on a classical theme. *Cognitive Science* 14: 355-384.

van Leusen, N. 1994. The Interpretation of Corrections. In P. Bosch & R. van der Sandt (Eds.), *Focus and Natural Language Processing*. vol. 3. Heidelberg: IBM.

van Rooy, R. 2004. Relevance and bidirectional OT. In: R. Blutner & H. Zeevat (Eds.), *Optimality Theory and Pragmatics*. New York: Palgrave/MacMillan.

van Rooy, R. 2004. Signalling games select Horn strategies. *Linguistics and Philosophy* 27: 493-527.

Vogel, R. 2004. Remarks on the Architecture of OT Syntax. In: R. Blutner & H. Zeevat (Eds.), *Optimality Theory and Pragmatics*. New York: Palgrave Macmillan.

Westerståhl, D. 1985. Determiners and Context Sets. In J. van Benthem & A. G. B. ter Meulen (Eds.), *Generalized Quantifiers in Natural Laguage*. Dordrecht: Foris.

Wexler, K., & Chien, Y.-C. 1985. *The development of lexical anaphors and pronouns*. vol. 24: Stanford University.

Williams, E. 1997. Blocking and anaphora. *Linguistic Inquiry* 28: 577-628.

Wurzel, W. U. 1998. On markedness. *Theoretical Linguistics* 24: 53-71.

Zeevat, H. 1998. Contracts in the Common Ground. In: *Proceedings Twendial 1998*.

Zeevat, H. 2000. The asymmetry of optimality theoretic syntax and semantics. *Journal of Semantics* 17: 243-262.

Zipf, G. K. 1949. *Human behavior and the principle of least effort*. Cambridge: Addison-Wesley.

Index

abductive, 108
abduction, 109
abstract structure, 26, 27
acoustic representation, 25, 26
adverbial quantification, 84
anaphor(s), *see also* anaphora,
 20, 57, 59, 61, 64, 74, 79, 81,
 82, 83, 84
anaphora, 52, 57, 74, 78, 83, 96,
 anaphoric(al), 20, 54, 58, 59,
 60, 61, 62, 63, 69, 70, 71, 72,
 73, 74, 75, 78, 80, 81, 83, 91,
 92, 93, 94, 95, 138, 140
anaphorization, 20, 84, 85, 86
anomaly, 110, 111, 112
 anomalous, 104, 111, 112
 pragmatically anomalous, 111
antecedent, 61, 62, 68, 69, 72,
 73, 74, 75, 80, 81, 82, 83, 84,
 85, 86, 91, 123, 140
architecture of OT, 21-22,
argument structure, 19, 38, 70,
 84

arrow diagram, 93, 112, 113, 115
articulatory instructions, *see also*
 motor instructions, 25
articulatory system, 25, 27
artificial neurons, 12
auto-associative learning, 128

bidirectional Gradual Learning
 Algorithm (biGLA), 147
bidirectional optimization, 23,
 24, 52, 53, 55, 89, 90, 93, 115,
 116, 136, 141, 142, 148
bidirectional system, 52
bidirectional OT, 23, 24, 25, 26,
 55, 64, 90, 91, 93, 94, 95, 96,
 97, 99, 100, 106, 107, 110,
 113, 114, 117, 119, 130, 133,
 134, 135, 141, 148, 149
binding theory, 20, 136, 137, 138
blocking, *see also* lexical
 blocking, 23, 24, 97, 104, 105,
 110, 111, 113, 114, 115, 119,
 148, 149

semantically equivalent, 19, 112
semantics, 13, 14, 18, 19, 20, 22,
  29, 30, 31, 54, 55, 61, 63, 64,
  68, 70, 71, 70, 74, 83, 89, 90,
  96, 98, 99, 104, 106, 113, 117,
  153, 158, 159
set of constraints, 4, 5, 6, 11, 12,
  13, 48, 50, 51, 71, 82, 86, 90,
  148
speaker perspective, 22, 24, 39,
  55, 64, 90, 136
speakerís efforts, 23
specifier-head agreement, 37
stereotypical information, 31
stochastic evaluation, 118, 144
stochastic OT, 144, 145
strict dominance, *see also* strict
  domination, 124, 156, 158
strict domination, 13, 39, 158
strong bidirection, *see also*
  strong bidirectionality, 110,
  115, 116, 129
strong bidirectionality, 121, 128,
  147, 150
structural description, 39, 40, 41,
  49, 126, 127, 128
structural economy, 36, 44
subject-object asymmetry, 131
suboptimal, 6, 9, 10, 11, 40, 88,
  122, 125, 148
subsymbolic level, 13, 27, 159
super-optimal, 22, 23, 93, 95,
  114, 115, 118, 134, 135, 141,
  142
super-optimal form-meaning
  pair, 94, 135
super-optimal pair, 22, 23, 93,
  94, 114, 115, 134, 135, 141,
  149
supervised learning, 128, 129
surface form, *see also* surface
  structure, 18, 20, 41, 45, 48

surface structure, 19, 37
syllabification, 4, 5, 6, 18
syllable, 4, 6, 7, 8, 9, 10, 11, 12,
  16, 17, 18, 129
symbolic grounding, 29, 32
symbolic level, 13, 27, 159
syntactic movement, 14, 35, 41,
  51
syntax, 7, 13, 14, 15, 18, 19, 22,
  39, 52, 55, 59, 60, 64, 65, 70,
  90, 98, 113, 137, 138, 153, 158

tableau, 8, 9, 10, 15, 21, 47, 60,
  62, 81, 82, 86, 117, 118, 123,
  139, 140, 141
target grammar, 126, 127, 128,
  144
tensor product formation, 154,
  155
test of symmetry, 129, 145
topicality, 57
topic-referring subject, 123
total blocking, 113
total ranking, 125, 127, 143, 144
trigger, 65, 66, 73, 82 ., 116, 122,
  126, 128, 129, 159
truth-conditional content, 29, 99,
  118
truth-conditional meaning, 70
truth-functional, 19, 30, 107, 117
truth-functionally equivalent, 19
typological generalization, 132
typology by reranking, 12

UG, *see also* Universal
  Grammar, 122, 143
underlying form, 7, 18, 48, 109,
  128
underlying structure, 26, 127
underspecification, 159
unidirectional optimization, 141
Universal Grammar, 122, 126